Gateway to the Miraculous

Gateway to the Miraculous

Further Explorations in the Tao of Cheng Man-ch'ing

Wolfe Lowenthal

Frog, Ltd.
Berkeley, California

Gateway to the Miraculous
Further Explorations in the Tao of Cheng Man-ch'ing

Copyright © 1994 by Wolfe Lowenthal. No portion of this book, except for brief review, may be reproduced in any form without written permission of the publisher. For information contact Frog, Ltd. c/o North Atlantic Books.

Published by
Frog, Ltd.

Frog, Ltd. books are distributed by
North Atlantic Books
P.O. Box 12327
Berkeley, California 94701

Cover and all interior photographs by Kenneth Van Sickle
Cover and book design by Paula Morrison
Typeset by Catherine Campaigne
Printed in the United States of America by Malloy Lithographing

First Frog, Ltd. publication 1994

Library of Congress Cataloging-in-Publication Data
Lowenthal, Wolfe, 1939–
    Gateway to the miraculous : further explorations in the tao
of Cheng Man-Ch'ing / Wolfe Lowenthal.
        p.   cm.
    ISBN 1-883319-13-7
    1. T'ai chi ch'üan—Philosophy.   I. Title.
GV504.L67   1994
613.7'148—dc20   93-39498
                                                              CIP

2   3   4   5   6   7   8   9 / 98   97   96   95

For Julian

Acknowledgements

I want to thank Ken Van Sickle for his beautiful photographs, as well as his open and generous spirit. Additionally, there are a number of other fine Tai Chi teachers and students who have helped me with the book: Mark Hennessey, Myles MacVane, Caesar Pacifici, Nancy Perkins and her fine artistry, and my two constant pillars of support, Nicole Gregory and John Wolfe.

I also want to thank Ling-nyi Hsu, with whom I worked years ago on the translation of the Yang Cheng-fu material included in this book.

Last but not least, I thank my fellow students at the Long River Tai Chi Circle. Some helped me with the book, some with the computer, and all helped me learn more about Tai Chi Chuan.

Contents

Introduction

This book is a sequel to my first, *There Are No Secrets*. Like the previous book it is about my teacher, the great Cheng Man-ch'ing, the art of Tai Chi Chuan, and my experience as a student and teacher.

Professor Cheng said that Tai Chi was useful for health, relaxation, and self defense, in that order of importance. Once on the path we began to understand that overriding all the benefits is that Tai Chi Chuan is a *tao*, a way of living.

Cheng Man-ch'ing died in 1975. Due to his transcendent ability and radiant spirit his Simplified Yang-Style Tai Chi, the so-called "short form," is very popular in Taiwan, Malaysia and Singapore among other places. Additionally, because of Professor Cheng's role as a fountainhead for Tai Chi in this country, his is the most widely practiced style of Tai Chi Chuan in the United States and continues to grow in popularity as more people become aware of its benefits.

Professor said that if he had to choose one of all the arts and sciences he practiced, it would be Tai Chi, because "it has the most to do with relating to people." In that spirit, I hope to provide a tool that can help the internal exploration of those who study not only Tai Chi Chuan but all the arts based on the principle of being soft, loving, and peaceful.

The Ancients

If you can take the tension and hard stiff force out of your hands and arms, you can begin to relate to the ball of energy that permeates the Tai Chi form. The ball of energy is sometimes plastic and sometimes literally round, and feeling it throughout the form is a basic method of chi development.

Working to develop your *ch'i* can also be an aid in the day-to-day happenings of your life. It's very valuable to continue working with this energy outside of the form. For instance, when you're uptight, the ball of energy will not be present. Your sense of the *ch'i* cannot coexist with tension. So, if you find yourself in a situation that makes you angry or fearful, get the feeling of *ch'i* back and then try to deal with the situation. If you can't relax into your *ch'i*, you'll only be able to address a situation from an uptight place where you won't be able to do any good.

Carl Jung tells the story of a student who came to a rabbi and said, "In the olden days there were people who saw the face of God. Why don't they, any more?"

The rabbi replied, "Because nowadays no one can stoop so low."

Professor often used to say, in a similar vein, "In ancient times people used to know the *Tao*."

The ancients were not learned, they did not know sophisticated definitions. They did not know the "meaning" of things, as when a parent tells a child, "That is a tree," as if that term, that definition, were the summation of the tree's reality.

The ancients may not have known its Latin designation, but they were not separate from the tree, or from the animals and the earth. They knew how to be in harmony and balance, which foods were good, which plants had curative powers. They knew movements and dances for health and energy.

They knew affection and love—they knew the face of God.

Knowledge and understanding of our *ch'i* can lead us back to this sense of the sacred and our true relationship to ourselves and the world.

Yang Cheng-fu

Cheng Man-ch'ing revered his teacher, Yang Cheng-fu. He talked about him often, about his mastery and teaching of Tai Chi Chuan. Recently I've begun to reexamine some earlier work I did on the writing of Yang Cheng-fu and its interrelationship with the teaching of his great and loyal student, Cheng Man-ch'ing.

Professor Cheng was a most highly cultivated, educated man. As Bob Smith wrote in *Chinese Boxing, Masters and Methods*, "Professor Cheng's eyes were very high." He was not a part of the low-class, rough Chinese martial arts scene. He was a university professor who created and exhibited traditional painting and calligraphy. He was also a famous physician, and studied and wrote extensively on the classics of Chinese philosophy.

Yang Cheng-fu, on the other hand, had the reputation of being a simple man, an uneducated fighter and carouser. However, his "writings," whether his own or, what is more likely, the work of others recording his words, reveal a different image—a delicate sensibility that equals Professor Cheng's in epitomizing the softness of Tai Chi Chuan as well as its spirituality.

It was the "tough guy" side of Yang Cheng-fu that Professor would often talk about—how he once asked his teacher to play Push Hands and Yang Cheng-fu threw him across a courtyard and into a wall with such force that the young Cheng Man-ch'ing lay paralyzed on the ground.

Yang Cheng-fu walked over and looked down at him. "Get up," he demanded.

Professor looked up at him but could not speak.

"Hmmmphhh! Then lay there!" And he stalked off.

Professor said he lay in the courtyard all day until feeling finally came back into his body.

Harsh, often injuring his students, and at the same time in touch with the qualities of the art that have the depth of the *Tao*, Yang Cheng-fu was a synthesis of the fierceness and gentleness of Tai Chi Chuan:

> As for the head, there are four ideas: The mind, like the universe itself, should have space, room enough to receive and contain anything.
>
> It should have the quality of deep awareness and alertness.
>
> It should be as if balancing something on the head while at the same time as if the top of the head were suspended from above.
>
> There should be the quality of inner energy.
>
> Taken together, these four ideas mean that the mind should be light and spacious, having the quality of perpetual alertness so that the spirit will rise and the inner energy emanate through the top of the head.
>
> The head should be straight to let the spirit rise. It should only be a thought, a function of the mind without physical effort, or else your neck will be stiff and the *ch'i* won't be able to circulate. Without relaxed application of these four ideas, it will be difficult for the spirit to rise and the body to achieve total alertness.
>
> The eyes express the spirit. When the spirit is present in the eyes, it may at times compensate for deficiencies in move-

ment and position. The eyes should focus levelly ahead and follow the movements of the body.*

Professor Cheng often talked about the position of the head, "as if pressing up against heaven," "as if being suspended by the pigtail" worn by Chinese during the Manchu dynasty. He said that, while there are a number of good images for the head position, he especially recommended the idea of "hanging" because it counteracted the tendency to hold the head stiffly in place.

He also had a grave warning for his students: if the head and spine were not kept straight, one could practice for thirty years and it would come to nothing.

Only once do I recall Professor Cheng referring to the way "spirit" can compensate for deficiencies in technique. He was referring to the unsurpassed "martial spirit" of the great Herman Kauz. The power of the spirit may also be why Professor taught that in Push Hands one should not look into the opponent's eyes. If we understand energy, we can ignore the power of the opponent's eyes and deal clearly with their total energy statement.

The mouth should be closed, but not tightly; the breathing should be natural. If you find saliva accumulating in your mouth, swallow it, don't spit it out.

Professor Cheng said that this accumulation of saliva refers to thin, watery saliva, not the thick, viscous sort which is not to be retained. Professor called swallowing the thin type of saliva better than the best medicine. In fact, his very important first advice on beginning the form—positioning the tip of the tongue at the place where the teeth and the

---

*Excerpted from "Ten Important Points for Practicing Tai Chi Chuan" by Yang Cheng-fu.

upper palate meet—is to nurture the accumulation of saliva, which has a role in the circulation of the *ch'i*. Professor also advised students whose mouth is dry to run the tip of the tongue up over the upper teeth and gums, with the mouth closed, to facilitate the flow of the thin saliva.

The quality of the mind's spaciousness, "like the universe itself" is a predominant theme in the teaching of Yang Cheng-fu. In Push Hands, being neutral is standing on the ground of victory. In principle, the one without the preconception—either to attack or retreat—will be the victor.

This absence of preconception, as well as not being judgmental, is where all of us can join the divine element in ourselves. Judgement comes from a sense of separation—myself from the other—but if we could see with the all-encompassing eyes of the universe where everything is One, who would be there to judge, and who is to be judged?

On the other hand, there is Professor Cheng's Confucian model of the spirit of Tai Chi Chuan: a scale with a balanced person in the center acting as the instrument for the opponent's destruction, depending on their imbalance, their acting out of greed or aggression.

> For the shoulders: Loosen the chest. Only then will the *ch'i* easily sink into the *tan tien* [literally, "field for the immortality elixir," approximately an inch below the navel]. When your chest is held up and puffed out, your *ch'i* will stuff up the chest cavity, causing your body to be top heavy and lose stability. Then the weight will have the quality of floating rather than being able to take root.
>
> Pull up the spine, loosening the joints between the vertebrae. Let the *ch'i* rise from the *tan tien*, along the spine, in company with the breath. In fact, if you can loosen your chest, you will naturally pull up your spine, and if you can

pull up the spine, your inner energy—initiated from a point between the shoulder blades—can be released without effort. Only in developing this kind of inner energy will you become a true Tai Chi player.

For Yang Cheng-fu the major defect in the practice of Tai Chi Chuan is "floating." Relaxation enables the practitioner to sink and tap the energy of the ground. Tension *X* works in the opposite way. If you are "uptight," you will be disconnected from the ground.

Professor said, "Be like a small child." The energy of a small child is centered in the abdomen, and the weight sinks. There is a sense in which we are born into the earth and then, as we get older and progressively more hard and tense, we float away. Reversing this process is one of the goals of Tai Chi. One of the problems with hard, stiff force (*li* energy) as opposed to soft energy (*chin*) is that the very nature of hard force disconnects the user from the ground. Only relaxation can sink.

As for "pulling up the spine," one should be careful not to exaggerate the idea. There are many practitioners who overdo "loosening the chest" to the extent that they appear misshapen, like a hunchback. There is obviously tension in the extreme rounding of the back and depressing the chest. Professor said that the idea of the thing is more to let go of the tendency to puff up the chest—the attitude of pride—rather than a forceful pushing in.

Allowing the breath to lead the *ch'i* up the spine is secondary to the most important idea in Tai Chi Chuan: centering the *ch'i* and heart-mind in the *tan tien.* *X*

Initially one should concentrate on putting the *ch'i* into the *tan tien*. It's the reason Professor withheld certain techniques, such as circulating and patterning the movement of the *ch'i* until this foundation work is accomplished.

First put the *ch'i* in the *tan tien*. You will begin to feel it accumulating and, at a certain point, it will begin to circulate in company with the heart-mind. The process of the circulation as outlined by Yang Cheng-fu: Inhale and allow the *ch'i*, in the company of the breath, to go from the *tan tien* to the base of the spine, then up the spine to the top of the head. To accomplish this, the breath must be long, thin, slow, and quiet.

Then, on the exhale, the *ch'i* is led from the top of the head back down to the place where "the tip of the tongue and the upper palate meet," down the throat and back to the *tan tien*. One breath up, one breath down.

As for the so-called "pattern" of the movement of the *ch'i* with that of the Tai Chi form, Professor would only describe it in general terms: When the form rises or expands, the *ch'i* fills up; when the form sinks or contracts the *ch'i* empties out. Thinking once again of the breath leading the *ch'i*—"As a horse leads a chariot"—inhale when the form rises or expands, exhale when it falls or contracts. Imagine a balloon, filling with air to expand, releasing air as it contracts. It should be noted that the pattern of the breath and *ch'i* movement with the form is the opposite of the way it would occur were one to use "external," hard energy in practicing.

"Initiating energy from between the shoulder blades," the last part of Yang Cheng-fu's comments on the shoulders, is part of a range of ideas on releasing the inner energy. Professor Cheng elaborated on the process of releasing internal energy: Energy is transferred from the rear foot to the front foot, then up the front leg and up the spine to the point between the shoulder blades. From there it emerges from the hand opposite the weighted leg—this in the so-called "70 percent–30 percent" postures, where 70 percent of the weight rests on the front leg and 30 percent on the rear. This process will take place if the practitioner has achieved a level of rootedness, softness, and one-pieced-ness. The release of energy through this pathway takes place in an instant. Very little of it can be seen by the inexperienced observer; nothing much will move, certainly not the hands and arms; there will be a slight gathering in the legs before the release, and then a coming forward, but most of the process is internal and invisible.

Once, in the early 1970s, when Professor Cheng was away on one of his trips back to Taiwan, a self-proclaimed expert on Tai Chi came to New York and gave a demonstration attended by a number of students of Tai Chi Chuan, including students of Cheng Man-ch'ing.

"If you were wise," the expert informed us, "you would study with me." He said that Cheng Man-ch'ing's technique was obviously inferior because Cheng's rear leg did not extend when he released energy. "How can you release energy," he exclaimed, "without there being a pushing off with the back leg?"

His conclusions seemed obvious to him, but after testing his abilities, the students of Cheng Man-ch'ing were unconvinced. While demonstrating Push Hands, he was rudely pushed and banged his head against the wall. Soon after, he left town in poor health while we remained to deepen our investigation of the subtle power of Cheng Man-ch'ing's technique.

One aspect of it is that the initial energy transference, from rear leg to front leg, does not occur with a straightening of the back leg. The energy is transferred beneath

9

the ground without any obvious pressing-up and straight-ening-out of the back leg.

Professor said that the form, "Fair Lady Weaving at the Shuttle" is the posture with which to practice the technique of releasing energy. At the final moment, with the hips squaring to the corner and the weight shift nearly complete, think internally of energy going from rear leg to front, up the front leg, out the point in the back between the shoulder blades, and into the lower hand opposite the weighted foot.

The point between the shoulder blades is one of the few places in the body described by Professor as being open, where it is physically impossible to put hard force. In this sense its "openness" makes it vulnerable to drafts and chill, which must be guarded against. The fullness of the back—lifting the spine and releasing the chest—enables the practitioner to develop the power of this insubstantial spot between the shoulder blades.

Among Tai Chi players there is often confusion about the difference between *ch'i* and the so-called "inner energy." That which is used to provide the great power of a correct Tai Chi push is not *ch'i* but *chin*, the inner energy. This inner energy is the energy system consistent with the *ch'i*, unlike the other form of energy—*li*, hard or so-called "external" energy—which is inconsistent with the *ch'i*. The *ch'i* operates through softness and pliability. A body that is hard blocks the flow of the *ch'i*; an organism without flexibility is in the condition of the absence of *ch'i*, which is death. We could say that *chin* is the way, the *tao*, of the *ch'i*.

This is not to say that it's impossible to send forth one's *ch'i*. There used to be a genre of Chinese film, lurid costume dramas depicting the ancient times, with a lot of sword fighting, *"kung fu"* and melodramatic plots. Occasionally the hero of one of these films, with the aid of primitive special effects, would stretch out his palm and a wave of laser-like, red energy would stream forth and blow apart a boulder. This image romanticizes a real, very high level development of *ch'i*.

I recall one time when Professor Cheng was fencing with an especially fierce opponent who could overpower his fellow students, but whom Professor continually warned about his hardness. Suddenly Professor's sword sprang off his opponent's and struck the student with a resounding crack across the forehead. In all the time I studied with him it was the only time I witnessed him causing injury—or at least it seemed certain that he had.

In the split-second while everyone looked on in shock, Professor dropped his sword and sprang at his stunned opponent, clasping his palm forcefully against the man's forehead, holding him behind the head with his other hand. He stood there for perhaps a minute. The student later described the sensation as "deep heat." When the student was released, there was a barely visible, thin red line across his forehead, which soon disappeared.

Professor said that this business of sending *ch'i* forth from his hands for healing was too draining. He much preferred the use of herbs.

Actually, There Is a Secret

"There are no secrets in the Tai Chi Chuan that I am teaching you," said Professor Cheng, "but if there *were* a secret, it is that the <u>mind moves the *ch'i*</u>."

Sometimes he would say, "There are no secrets in this Tai Chi Chuan, but if there was a secret, it is that the hands don't move." This was yet another one of those times when I initially thought he was contradicting himself, only to realize later that in both cases he was saying the same thing: "The hands don't move," and "The mind moves the *ch'i*" are the same, and the secret of our Tai Chi Chuan.

"The hands don't move." It is rather the mind, or more precisely, the idea that directs the waist to produce the movement. <u>The energy only emerges from the hands, which move from the waist like spokes on the hub of a wheel.</u>

"The waist is the commander," it says in the Tai Chi classics, and the hands should submit totally to the command of the waist—never moving independently. Basically, the waist moves, the hands do not. There is nothing more characteristic of Professor Cheng's Tai Chi Chuan. It is the opposite of hard-style boxing in which the hand and arm move from the shoulder, independent of the body. Even other styles of Tai Chi Chuan have more independent movement of the hand. The idea, then, directs the waist and so "The mind moves the *ch'i*."

The implications of this "secret" go far beyond the special skill of a unique form of boxing. It is important to understand that this "*ch'i*" of which we speak is part of the cosmic *ch'i*, the primal energy of the universe. In Professor Cheng's words, "The same *ch'i* that moves in our bodies is the *ch'i* that moves the stars in the heavens."

To say that the Idea, the intuitive, creative power of our heart-mind, directs the *ch'i* is to say that our heart-mind has in its control the essential creative force of the universe.

To the boxer it means that we can be as quick, direct, and penetrating as thought. This is the basis for the statement in the Tai Chi classics: "He starts before I do, but I arrive first."

It is why a seventy-five-year-old Tai Chi expert is more than a match for a group of younger, stronger men. Willful muscular energy is like a horse and carriage compared to the rocketship speed of thought.

But it just begins with the boxer. This secret goes far beyond martial art. It stands at the gateway to the miraculous.

Professor used to say that a sage sitting alone in his room can change the world. Our minds can control the energy that makes up the fabric of life, *all* the stuff of our inner and outer reality. This is not magic or "New-Age" fantasy.

That the heart-mind has in its control the essential creative force of the universe does not mean we can readily tap into its power. For most people—and for most martial artists—we are letting our hands do it, in a pathetic expression of our egos' need to control, defend, and manipulate.

Even so, despite our lack of faith in the true core of our power, it is operating anyway, in its fashion. The heart-mind doesn't go to sleep because we do not recognize it. It simply expresses our lack of faith by giving power to our faithlessness. That's how it operates. It will empower your love and creativity—or it will fuel your fear and destructiveness.

Tai Chi Chuan is the study of *Tao*, which is to say that it is the study of harmony.

The first stage of this study is the realization that we are responsible for our lack of harmony, for our own tension and fear. Disharmony, in a person or situation does not enter our lives from without. We create it from within. The great illusion of disempowerment is that the crises and difficulties of life in themselves are responsible for our disharmony. As Professor said, "A great mountain can collapse at your feet and you need not change countenance." We are in control. Not the ferocious attacker, not even death and dying; whether we react to those things with terror or with harmony is up to us, not them. There is nothing that in and of itself need destroy our sense of well-being.

We can change disharmony, transform tension into relaxation, fear into joy, illness into health. The power is in us, not in the situation nor in the other person.

Harmony is itself paradise. The "miraculous" element is the way that relaxation, well-being, and harmony allow the heart-mind to take control of and focus the greatness of the *ch'i*, the power of thought, and the effect that this can have in ourselves and in the world.

I'm Not a Hook—Why Do You Put Your Dead Meat on Me?

Translated in different ways, Yang Cheng-fu's warning, "Don't put your dead meat on me!" was described by Professor Cheng as being "a secret family transmission. It has a very deep meaning that requires careful study."*

Last year a senior student at the Long River Push Hands class remarked that he had witnessed a street fight and found the youthful speed, power, and hostility of the combatants a convincing argument against thinking of Tai Chi Chuan as a martial art.

"The only way you're going to be able to deal with guys like that," said the student, "is learn some Taekwando or, even better, get a gun."

This is an understandable, if mistaken, point of view. The art of Tai Chi Chuan, throughout its early stages—which can last a frustratingly long period of time—seems totally inadequate in dealing with a fast, strong, fierce aggressor.

But Cheng Man-ch'ing reminds us, "We are studying *Tao*. If this art were not useful against the fiercest attacker,

---

*Professor Cheng's *Thirteen Treatises*, North Atlantic Books, 1985

it would not be worthy of the name of Tài Chi Chuan. Therefore it would not be part of the true *Tao*."

In 1981, I was teaching Tài Chi Chuan at the Naropa Institute summer program in Boulder, Colorado. At the same time there was a serious student of Tài Chi Chuan in Boulder who was teaching a different style, and making quite a reputation for himself. This fellow—let's call him Richard—put much of his focus on application, the martial aspect of the art of Tài Chi Chuan, following what he says is the no-nonsense tradition of the teachers he met in China.

Before Richard left to study in China, we had been friendly. He was a pleasant if somewhat eccentric young guy who hung around for a brief time at Professor's school. A decade later in Boulder, though, our relationship had changed. We both had something to defend: Richard, as an outsider, the superiority of his training in China; myself, the teaching and the honor of Cheng Man-ch'ing.

All during that summer Richard and I never exchanged a word, eyeing each other like two stallions vying for supremacy. Then, one day toward the end of the summer, Myles MacVane came for a visit. Myles is a fellow student, an outstanding member of the Cheng Man-ch'ing family of teachers. Myles had also been acquainted with Richard in the old days and he told me an interesting tale.

Richard had once asked Myles to show him Professor's Push Hands, with which he was not familiar. In the course of Myles' instructing him, without warning Richard suddenly lifted his knee and struck Myles in the groin.

After rolling around on the floor for a couple of minutes, Myles got his breath back. "What are you doing?" he cried.

Richard explained that the martial arts he had learned in China was more serious stuff than what was being practiced in the United States. "In doing Push Hands one must be prepared for anything," he warned.

It was important information, so I began to study this point carefully.

A year later I gained some first-hand experience. I was visited by two Karate students, senior black belts who studied with another old fellow student, Min Pai. Min is a well known Karate instructor who initiates his advanced black belts into the basic techniques of Push Hands, and they wanted to practice with an experienced Tai Chi player.

Totally immersed as they were in hard-style martial art, their Push Hands lacked softness and sensitivity. They were not very good, but one of them taught me something of the same lesson Richard taught Myles.

After having neutralized his attacks without too much trouble, I decided to try a push. I easily got my hands onto his body, but I was surprised by his extreme and unTai Chi-like resistance, a quality of energy I wasn't used to, practicing as I did in the protected environment of a Tai Chi school.

In that split second, I pushed hard at his resistance, and my own body and energy became like his—dead meat. The next thing I knew he had launched both fists at the sides of my head. Since I had connected with his center and in the same moment he was being shoved off-balance, his attack could do no real harm, but it got my attention ringingly.

The rest of the round I was very careful never to lock my energy into his, not to become dead meat, and only to push when his center was totally vulnerable.

In the days, months, and decade since, my commitment to the art of my teacher has focused my attention on the meaning of the idea, "I'm not a hook—don't put your dead meat on me."

The same senior student at Long River school whose misstatement I quoted above is also beginning to understand. Recently he said to a class of his juniors, "Push with the idea of defending, and neutralize with the idea of attack." An enlightened idea.

Softness provides the framework for sensitivity and alertness. If you are hard, you will be stiff. Remember the old slang word "stiff," meaning a corpse. Whenever you are hard and stiff, your awareness is like the narrowest tunnel vision, and you are vulnerable to anything outside that tunnel—kicks, punches, or pokes in the eye.

The function needs to be precise. Pushing or neutralizing correctly means that we should be able to use just a touch to send the opponent flying. We can't make a stiff, gross commitment of energy against an opponent and still have the reserve to maintain our protective field of concentration, which is alive and vital—the complete opposite of "dead meat."

Professor said that the key to learning Push Hands lies in the phrase, "Never use more than four ounces nor let more than four ounces build up on you." Stated another way, "Don't resist, don't insist." This is the method, the secret to developing the *tao* of self-defense in Tai Chi Chuan.

Referring to Yang Cheng-fu's transmission, "I'm not a hook—don't put your dead meat on me," Professor Cheng said, "It has a very deep meaning that requires careful study." We should seek to use all our creativity in our Tai Chi Chuan. If there is an energy or reality that frightens you, that seems overpowering, seek to create a vision of how your art can deal with that force. Then, with that vision as a goal, work to achieve it.

The Waist Is the Commander

Yang Cheng-fu said of the waist, "Let it be loose." "The waist" refers to the area between the hip joints, the center of which is the *tan tien*. The waist is the director of the whole body. Shifts of weight and other changes in movement are all motivated by the waist. If the waist can be loosened, the root will be stabilized and the inner energy will sprout from the feet. That's why it is said (in the Tai Chi classics), "The source of command is at the waist." When there are signs of instability, the cause can always be traced to the waist and legs.

Professor transmitted this to his students almost verbatim. Referring to push hands, he used to say that if you were being pushed, look for the source of the problem in the waist.

Some students of Professor have contributed their own ideas to the theme of "The waist is the commander:"

Mr. Liu Hsi-heng stresses the idea of "the popsicle." The practitioner should imagine shoulders, hips, and knees as part of a twin popsicle. In turning, the integrity of the popsicle should be maintained; the popsicle must not be broken.

William C. C. Chen has said that the classical statement of the waist being the commander can be a little misleading. According to William, it's more helpful to think of the thigh as the real commander, with the hips and waist following. He felt that people thinking of "the waist as the commander" were twisting rather than using their root.*

This is basically just a different way of looking at Liu Hsi-heng's popsicle. If you think of the thighs as the sticks and the hips and shoulders as the popsicle—all in one line—the only place from which you can turn the popsicle without splitting it is the thigh. In that sense, as William Chen says, "The thigh is the real commander."

Once, when he was studying with Cheng Man-ch'ing, Mr. Liu walked in on Professor Cheng while he was practicing alone. Professor was doing an exercise that Mr. Liu had never seen before. Without saying anything, Professor winked at Mr. Liu and continued what he was doing. That secret exercise gave Mr. Liu his insight into the idea of the popsicle, and forms the basis of his teaching of Tai Chi Chuan.

In its simplest form the exercise is a wonderful method of rooting. Put 100 percent of the weight on the back leg. Then turn the waist by dropping the knee and thigh of the front leg and folding into the groin area of the rear leg. Crucial to the exercise is that the sacrum must hang, the back be straight and the weight fall into the center of the foot. You can allow the arms to swing at the sides.

A good test of the correctness of the exercise is that ideally the rear knee should not move. However, as Professor Cheng was careful to point out, do not attempt to hold the rear knee in place. That would be a serious mistake. Work on the exercise and gradually, as your root and posture im-

---

*T'ai Chi magazine, June 1992.

prove, you will grasp the idea and the rear knee will stay in place.

Professor Cheng himself referred back to Yang Cheng-fu when he said that one of his teacher's real secrets in his oral teaching is, "The millstone turns but the axle doesn't turn."* Again, if you do the turning in Mr. Liu's popsicle exercise correctly, an imaginary line down the center of the body—the axle—will remain stable while the waist—the millstone—will turn around it.

Of course, this idea is not unique to "the popsicle" exercise but is central to all the turning in Tai Chi, the basis of the root and stability. Of the concept that "the millstone turns but the axle doesn't turn," Professor said, "Since I learned this I find improvement every day."

Thirteen Treatises.

Notes on the Sword

Professor Cheng said that the Tai Chi Chuan he practiced was like a tripod with three legs. This "tripod" is the thirty-seven-posture form, Push Hands, and the sword, which includes both the form and fencing. It is not the entirety of what he practiced. For example, there is the *Da Liu* exercise and the lance, both of which he taught to a few of his students. There were also some supplementary exercises, such as the "Eight Methods."

However, he said that the "tripod" makes up his Tai Chi Chuan. Everything else is secondary and to an extent limited.

His students were taught the form first, then Push Hands and last the sword—first form, then fencing. This is not to say that he considered any of the three more or less important; they are all equal.

Though he taught the sword last, fencing seemed to be his favorite of all. He once described himself as a "fire person" who was therefore especially attracted to the "fiery" nature of sword play. The one class that he really "took" along with his students—rather than standing apart and instructing—was the sword class. He seemed to sparkle with excitement as he chased a succession of desperate opponents around the room. He often ended up laughing and out of breath, which he said was a benefit of fencing unavailable in any other part of the *gung fu* (practice, discipline).

Initially the sword was a functional weapon. Professor said that in China, throughout much of its history, if a person strapped a sword on their back, that they really knew how to use, there was no place they couldn't go.

Someone once mentioned to him that in the play "Cyrano," the hero prevailed all alone against a force of a hundred men. He said that was no problem. Then he went into a corner of the room with his sword and pantomimed combat. He explained that if you position yourself correctly you can deal with an entire army, one man at a time. (He often made objectively absurd statements like this which, coming from him, seemed perfectly logical!)

With the invention of guns, of course, history moved past the ability of the master swordsman to make his way in the world unopposed. However, said Professor, the sword still has great value for us. Its most important value is as a method of *ch'i* development. A requirement of Tai Chi sword practice is to be able to send one's *ch'i* into the sword itself.

Everything about Professor's Tai Chi has at its core understanding and developing the "greatness of one's *ch'i*." There is little in our Tai Chi Chuan that surpasses the sword in demanding and developing the greatness of the *ch'i*.

A Tai Chi form can be thought of as a boat that is supported on the lake of one's *ch'i*. The greater the boat, the larger and deeper the lake necessary to support it. The sword form requires, as it develops, a very deep lake of *ch'i*. As you let go of hard force to support the weight and movement of the sword, you start to sense and develop a different kind of support—that of the root and the *ch'i*.

The critical step, as in every aspect of Tai Chi Chuan, is

to give up the hard force that is our programmed response to the task of dealing with this piece of metal or wood. Only after letting go of hardness can we be open, physically and mentally, to the more subtle energy of Tai Chi Chuan. First relax, and everything else will follow.

Another virtue of the sword lies in its fiery nature. There is more movement, more speed, leaping, twirling—the possibility of getting out of breath—it's a more directly aerobic exercise than any other part of our *gung fu*.

Its mobile quality is the essence of its function. Push hands is about fixed feet positions. The crucial work is done with the waist. With the sword, the lesson is how to gain positional advantage by moving the feet. The equivalent of what the waist does in Push Hands, the feet do in the sword practice.

The form and Push Hands are the "Chuan" of Tai Chi, the empty handed martial art. With the sword we take the first step of extending our understanding of Tai Chi principle to using a weapon, and therefore a tool of any kind. I remember one year when I was working on a construction crew for an old friend of mine, Jim Johnson. My job was rough carpentry—pounding long, heavy nails into very stubborn, hard wood. After a week I could hardly lift my arm. Thankfully, Jim took me aside. "Your problem," he said, "is that you're trying to do it all with your arm. You're not using your Tai Chi."

Once I grasped the principle—relaxing and using the ground, using the waist—the nails went in as if into butter instead of hard cement, to say nothing of eliminating the wear and tear on my poor arm.

The step from chuan, "empty hand," to the use of a weapon, or a tool, extends even further, to using Tai Chi principles, speaking in martial terms, in commanding a detachment of soldiers or an army. The writing of Vo Nguyen Giap, the great Vietnamese general who led the North Vietnamese army to victory first against the French and then the American armies reads like a textbook on Tai Chi Chuan. His basic principle was to yield to superior force, and consolidate one's attack against the opponents' weak areas—this is in itself the essence of the great polarity principle of Tai Chi Chuan.

Few of us are likely to use Tai Chi principles in the commanding of military forces, but we can lead any small or large group of people through extending the principles of Tai Chi Chuan.

Basically, the practice of the sword is doing the Tai Chi form with a sword in one's hand. The postures are similar, many of them nearly exactly the same. All the essential principles apply: relaxation, straightness, sinking; head, torso and waist moving as one piece; movements even and slow, neither speeding up nor slowing down.

But there are some unique elements to the sword form. First of all, one must be aware of the sword—of its weight, its balance point, its very *ch'i.*

Paradoxically, though the sword has real weight and substance, it should become as if weightless. There should be no drag; once the sword is in motion it should flow effortlessly. One should experience the sword like a living thing; you are both following and shaping it. And, as in my experience on the construction site, a sign that you're not using Tai Chi is when the arm and shoulder get tired or sore.

Much of the function of the sword, its martial application, depends on achieving the paradox of a weighty object becoming weightless, a lifeless tool becoming alive like a cat. With this quality the Tai Chi sword is able to match much lighter Western fencing swords.

Another difference between the sword and the regular Tai Chi form has to do with the eyes. In the regular form, the nose is in line with the belly button, and the gaze flows straight forward. In the sword form, the nose and belly button remain in alignment but the eyes move to follow the sword, or more precisely the active element at each moment in the form—sometimes the blade, sometimes the point, sometimes the butt, sometimes even the opposite hand. It has to do with hand-eye coordination. As a student once said, "People who are good with the sword really have great aim."

Another characteristic of the Tai Chi sword is that the left hand reinforces the right hand in which the sword is usually held. Since the basic principle of internal energy is "full hand opposite weight-bearing foot," and since the weight is always shifting, the left hand shares function with the right, even though it rarely holds the sword.

Grip the sword firmly but without tension. Think of the hand and sword as being one piece. A special point: in turning the sword, rotate the forearm, not the wrist. A secret of the sword is to have the idea that the two long bones in the forearm that connect the elbow to the wrist should not cross.

Even the tassel on the sword plays a part. There are functional uses of the tassel but, most important, it will tell the practitioner whether his movements are correct or not. If the hand and arm are making the movement—as they should not—the tassel will bind up around and the hand and sword, almost as if to say, "Stop that silly stuff." When the sword is used in the right way, the tassel flows behind smoothly.

As with the form, motivate the movement with the legs and waist, not with the arm. A goal of swordplay is to combine our Tai Chi quality of stable, heavy rootedness with rapid movement. Be as solid as a tree but as quick as a cat. Work to develop a sense of root even when the form has you leaping off the ground.

The *ch'i* sets the sword in motion. After that, like a hawk sailing on wind currents, let the sword ride the currents of gravity and centrifugal force.

Fencing

Professor Cheng once told a story of how, after decades of studying and practicing the art of calligraphy, he finally had to confront the fact that he had adopted a false model and that his own work was worthless. For all those years he had emulated a famous calligrapher whose stylish work he finally realized was decadent; it lacked straightness, simplicity, and solidity. He had to start all over again, from scratch, to develop calligraphy reflecting the integrity, the *tao*, that he now understood to be at the core of the art.

A few years ago I came to a similar realization about my approach to the sword. Concentrating on defeating my fellow students, I had come to rely on quickness and reflexes. I finally realized that these were hard-style virtues, the attributes of youth, and since I wasn't getting any younger, my skill, such as it was, was deteriorating, like a forty-year-old baseball player no longer able to hit the fastball. I had not been doing Tai Chi Chuan.

I had to start over from scratch. I thought back to the old man—what it felt like to fence with him. There was none of the reliance on speed and aggressiveness that I felt in myself and my fellow students. Professor's spirit was calm and relaxed, and yet he was in complete control of your sword. The most interesting feeling was that you couldn't resist or attack him even if you wanted to. He always seemed like a mighty river flowing through some part of your sword. The only option seemed to be to try to get away from there, to escape, but he stayed on you and inevitably you were cut.

This ability to attach, to control the other's sword while simultaneously sensing and attacking the weakness in it, were elements completely missing in my own *gung fu*.

When I took to heart Professor's words, "Study the form; it has meaning!" it was a critical insight in helping me deepen my understanding of Push Hands.

"Study the form; it has meaning!" is also true of the sword. In Push Hands, however, "study the form" applies to "*Peng, Lu, Chi, Ahn*," the four positions of "Grasping the Sparrows Tail." In sword practice one must "study" the entirety of the form to understand its "meaning"—ability in fencing.

In fencing the hand is the primary target. Professor explained that since Tai Chi is a Taoist art, we would first seek to disarm the opponent before inflicting more serious harm. However, having the hand as the target is very practical. Unless he's a complete idiot, your opponent's hand will be the closest part of his body to you. All other things being equal, if you are after my heart and I am after your hand, I have a tremendous advantage—my target is a lot more accessible than yours.

This points up another aspect of fencing: it does not pay to be greedy. When you begin to understand the Tai Chi sword, you will experience the advantage of neutrality. An opponent whose goal is to take your life rather than disarm you will do very badly if you are able to stick to his sword and to his energy. He will invariably try to do too much, leaving you a much shorter path to destroying him than he has to take to destroy you.

A basic strategy in fencing is to have the point of your sword at the hilt of the opponent's sword, while at the same time his point is far away from your hilt. Professor Cheng recommended an exercise to develop this skill.

Rest the point of the sword on the ground. Then use the waist to move the hilt from side to side allowing the point to stay fixed in the same spot. Once you get the feeling for it—and the point does not move—let the point come off the ground. Then do the exercise with the point staying fixed in space while the hilt continues to move in broad circles. This is the foundation for Tai Chi fencing: have the point stay in the same spot while the hand holding the hilt moves anywhere.

An inferior fencer, someone using hard force, will do exactly the opposite. In the heat of fencing, their hand—the hilt—will stay fixed and hard, and they will whirl the point around in a broad circle. It creates a kind of whirlpool effect. A superior fencer will simply allow the point of their sword to go down the "whirlpool" until they cut the wrist.

Like every other part of Tai Chi, it's not in the hand or arm. This is the sword version of Professor's "secret": "The hands don't move." The arm is relaxed; move the sword by moving the waist, generating the movement from the legs.

It's also necessary to balance the sword so that it floats effortlessly as it moves from side to side. This is the key to the "great aim" of the Tai Chi fencer.

Don't get carried away with the ability to cut the opponent before they cut you. We must understand that the sword is not electrified. The opponent will not die if they are touched.

There must be energy and focus behind the cut or stab (even if that energy is not fully expressed so that you don't injure your partner).

Of even greater importance, it accomplishes little to cut an opponent a split second before they cut you. In reality even a fatal cut would not necessarily prevent an opponent from fatally cutting you in return. Often a fencer will congratulate himself for cutting his opponent's chest an instant before his own hand would have been amputated. If you were a swordsman in actual combat, you would have a very short career if you depended on that kind of "victory."

So, bearing in mind the reality that underlies the sword, the only correct way to cut an opponent is to be sure that in the next moment they cannot cut you. This is the real art of fencing: to cut the opponent while at the same time being in total control of their sword, ensuring that they cannot lash out at you as they are being defeated.

In Sun-Tzu's classic *The Art of War* it says, "Know the opponent and know yourself, and in a thousand battles you will not be defeated." You must understand the balance of your sword while at the same time sensing the yin and yang in the opponent's sword. As in Push Hands, a hard spot will mean there is a counter line of energy, a soft spot that cannot be defended. But while in Push Hands these hard and soft spots are at different points in the opponent's body, they will be nearly at the same place in the opponent's sword.

You must be able to "hear" and stick to the opponent's energy. Then you will be able to control the "soft" spot on their sword, leaving them helpless and open to your cut. The ability to sense and control the "soft" spot is also the basis of the idea stated in the Tai Chi classics of "deflecting a thousand pounds with four ounces."

Generally, it's important to stick to the opponent's sword, but if you "hear" the other person's energy and their intent, you can even detach with impunity. If the opponent is in the process of blocking you, their mind and energy are locked so you can detach and cut them before they can respond. If they are running away, their energy is in retreat, and you can often detach and cut them safely. Still, safety comes from being in vital contact with your opponent's sword, so if you detach you must be certain that their energy and intent are not a threat.

In Push Hands you neutralize your opponent by moving the waist, not the hands. If your waist is rigid and you try to do it with your hands and arms, your technique is bad. With the sword the feet perform the function that the waist performs in Push Hands. You can't be lazy in fencing; you have to move your feet. On the other hand, a problem with many fencers is that they've seen too many *"samurai"* movies. The florid tango of movement when fencers are out of sword range is all a mind game; it's about "psyching" the opponent, if it has any relevance at all. But when the swords connect, if one understands energy, there is no time for psychological games and irrelevant posturing. Each moment, each step, each small degree of advantage becomes too important.

There are a range of secondary, technical factors that a fencer must be aware of. For instance, the guard on the hilt protects against the opponent's sword sliding down the blade. The handle of the sword can be grabbed, so in close combat be aware of this possibility.

My favorite of all Professor's many pointers in fencing is, "Don't raise the sword over your head. If you do, the ten thousand sword fairies will laugh at you." When you start to understand the sword, the idea becomes pretty obvious, but listening for those giggling sword fairies is a nice way of remembering the old man who was "never tired of learning."

The *Chung Yung*

When Professor Cheng would play push hands with students, he would often take us by the hand, as if he were escorting a child across the street. He also seemed innocent, so it was as if we were both small children.

But there was an overpowering heaviness in his touch, a weightedness, that buckled my knees. It took me a while to get used to it; at first I would blush with embarrassment whenever he did it. Later I came to accept it as an expression of what seemed to be an almost alien nature.

The recent birth of my son Julian gave me a fresh insight. One of the first things he did was take my hand. Though Julian's touch lacks Professor's weight, there is something of the same *ch'i*. His touch does not hesitate, argue with itself, or send its energy in circles. Julian's grip, like Professor's, is pure and irresistible. They are forces of nature; it is the rest of us that are alien.

Professor once said, "I do not aspire to being a living Buddha. All I want is to become a human being." The humility in the statement is obvious; it is also quite ambitious.

Professor described an idea translated into English as "sincerity" which, he said, is the understanding of what it means to "be a human being"—understanding not in the abstract but in flesh and blood, and in the heart. Essentially, it is the realization of one's basic human nature.

It also extends beyond the individual. It allows him to reach the *Chung Yung*.

The basis of Confucian philosophy, the *Chung Yung* is commonly translated as "The Doctrine of the Mean." Professor Cheng explained that the phrase literally has the following meaning: *"Chung"* is "straight, not leaning." *"Yung"* means "that which does not change." Taking them together, *"Chung Yung"* represents immutable straightness. In a world of constant change, it is the one thing that remains unchangeable.

Professor considered himself a student of Confucius, so he wrote and talked in depth about the principle of *Chung Yung* in a philosophical sense; but he also had a lot to say about its relationship to Tai Chi Chuan.

The *Chung Yung* is the line that connects heaven to earth, said Professor. For the Tai Chi player, it must be constant; you must never lose it. As you shift weight in the form, or as someone tries to throw you off-balance in Push Hands, you must maintain the straightness that connects heaven to earth: head pressed up against heaven, spine absolutely straight—each vertebra sitting on top of the next like a stack of Chinese chess pieces—and the sacrum hanging straight down, as if "the weight of the ten thousand things" were hanging from the base of the sacrum.

One day, for a special lecture on *Chung Yung*, Professor Cheng brought a scale to school. It was the kind that's used in apothecary shops in Chinatown. A bar hangs from a string; on one side of the bar is a hook from which a tray is suspended. On the other side of the bar is a weight which is moved back and forth on the bar until the level is balanced, thereby determining the weight of the herbs in the tray.

How many times had I gone to a little shop in China-town where I watched the apothecary use such a scale to fill Professor's prescription? Now Professor was using it for a different kind of prescription:

> My feeling is that the teachings of Confucius can be put into one phrase: humanity and benevolence—the principle of being a human being. Confucius is not talking about religion. He is talking about learning, about education.
>
> Confucius tried in his daily life to attain *Chung Yung*. But it is most difficult to practice. Confucius said that if he could attain *Chung Yung* in the morning he would be willing to die that night.
>
> The *Chung Yung* has a set idea to it. If the student contemplates the pattern of reality—both the seen and the unseen—it becomes apparent why one must have grasped the principle of *Chung Yung* to fully understand the meaning of Tai Chi.
>
> How is it that *Chung Yung* has such an important relationship to Tai Chi Chuan? Gradually, gradually, you'll come to understand. It has to do with balance and the center of gravity.
>
> The most important part of the *Chung Yung* is the center of gravity. The next most important part is the precise timing in the center—Shr Jung (the name Professor chose for his Tai Chi school). There's an important relationship between center of balance and precise timing. They are mutually interlocking.
>
> I've been in America for ten years. There are those who have studied with me for thirty, forty years. No one has come up to my ability. It has to do with the center of balance.
>
> It absolutely has nothing to do with strength. I have no strength with which to attack you.
>
> A good way to help understand the center of balance is with a Chinese scale: if we put something heavy on the hook

it will bring the level bar down. In order to maintain the level, you have to move the heavy weight on the left side, the counter-balance. The meaning of this counter-balance is "power" and "control." It is this counter-balancing weight that always keeps the balance by moving in and out.

In order to find the center of balance we depend on the counter-balance. If you control the counter-balance, you maintain your own stability.

The *ch'i* never stops. It is perpetually in motion, perpetually changing. That which allows you to maintain your balance in the presence of change is control over the counter-balance. Holding to the center without counter-balance is like holding to one point stubbornly. It is the same as being stuck.

I have control or power when I have control of the counter-balance weight. The idea of *Chung Yung* we talk about is like having control of the counter-balance weight.

My Tai Chi school has to do with this: "balance." (In his talk that day, Professor spoke this single word in English.)

The most important, the highest principle is that of balance. No matter what happens, always be balanced.

What word is contrary to happiness? The opposite of happiness? Think it over ...

The word is "wrong," in the sense of overdoing it, being too extreme. In this life there is happiness on one hand, and on the other overdoing things.

We are not saints. When we overdo things, we must correct ourselves. What is in the past is already gone.

Rooted in his ancient philosophy, Professor Cheng allowed his imagination to leap forward to our technological era:

The *Chung Yung* is a very, very difficult thing to discuss, a knotty problem. No one has clarified it to the point of comprehension. What is so difficult? Actually it is very simple. How to be a human being? This is what's difficult.

Chinese say, "Throughout the world, we're all human beings," but the way we act as human beings today is not the same as people acted in the past.

It takes one day to go from China to America. Simple, perhaps too simple. In former times it might have taken years. The world has shrunk to the size of an egg. For instance, here we are today. Tomorrow we could be on the other side of the earth. We can record what we say and take it to the TV station and the whole nation can see it. We can talk to people on the moon. We are a very different generation than any that came before. We cannot have a narrow view of how to live as a human being. All mankind is in the human family.

Benevolence is the center and heart of all that heaven and earth create. To have searched for benevolence, come upon and possessed it, is to have hit precisely the target of all human seeking.

Professor Cheng was in so many ways like a child, direct and innocent. Yet he also had a great sophistication. He took the *Chung Yung* and held to it as he turned with the world across oceans of the past into an alien present that for all its technology is desperately searching for its lost center.

A Short History
of a Tai Chi Player

I was born premature and was a sickly child. All through childhood I was undersized and underweight, generally the smallest kid in the class. Though I felt inferior because of my size, I had an intuition that life in general and my life in particular were destined to be marvelous. It was the 1940s, a time of wonderful struggle, triumph, and hope in America. As it does for so many children, my life seemed to sparkle.

Then came the dark ages, the fifties, my adolescence and early adulthood. The fifties were a horrendous decade, a time when people were not in touch with their feelings toward themselves or one another. Boys and young men presented facades of "tough" and "cool" to one another, and women were seen as objects to be conquered. The idea that a man could talk to a woman in depth, with openness and honesty, did not exist. The very sense that there existed an openness and honesty that could be shared was absent. In the fifties, what young people tended to carry inside was the desperate need to hide our feelings in general, and what we felt about ourselves in particular.

What we held to be important was being liked and looking good. It was a time of emptiness and sterility, a spiritual wasteland. I can remember sitting alone at college, reading Lao Tzu, and having the clear intimation that life was supposed to be a happy and serene reflection of the words I was reading, but that somehow I had gotten myself trapped in a nightmare world, and that I had no idea how to escape. I had no idea how to live a life consistent with the spirit of the book I had open in front of me.

By the early sixties the times already were "a-changing" —at different speeds for different people. McCarthyism, which had a lot to do with the "spiritual wasteland," was on the way out (though personally, like so many of my peers, I was oblivious to the political currents that had affected my life); openness and change were in the air.

As yet I had no vision of that change. I graduated from college, married as I believed I was supposed to do, served my obligatory time in the army, and emerged ready to realize my childhood dream of a life of fun and fulfillment. I got a part-time job, and sat down the rest of the day to write the Great American Play, the play that everyone said showed such "promise."

Three years later I was at the same job—and the same play. A producer had been interested, but as I kept rewriting, changing it without improving it, his interest waned. I had the growing suspicion that my personal lack of depth and insight had doomed my writing. I had never really lived, so how could I write? Topping it all off, my marriage was as drab and joyless as the rest of my life. I felt absolutely stuck.

Early in the sixties I had grown a beard—a polite, hesitant little goatee that feebly expressed my vague rebellion against conformity.

One night I was out with some friends, and we decided to go to a local polka club. I was sitting at the table when suddenly a beery patron reached down and grabbed my beard. He laughed, winked at his friends, and walked away.

All that night and for weeks after, I felt I was about to explode. I realized I had to do something to deal with the overwhelming feelings of frustration and powerlessness. I chose to study Karate rather than get psychiatric help, and gained a degree of stabilization. Still, I was going nowhere, and I felt trapped.

By the mid sixties the Vietnam War had started to pick up steam, accelerating the changes in society. Cracks began to appear in the prison walls of the "dark ages" that American society had fallen into after the end of World War II.

As for my personal psychic prison, the turning point arrived. I discovered Professor Cheng Man-ch'ing, a man whose being radiated honesty, power, and joy.

"To study Tai Chi Chuan means to learn to relax," were his first words to my beginners' class, and it was his constant message. "Relax. Let go of all tension, all hardness. Be soft. Hardness is the discipline of death; softness is the discipline of life. So, wherever you identify tension or hardness, let it go. Relax completely. This is what it means to study Tai Chi Chuan."

Leaving my first class in 1967, I felt as if I were floating on air.

From deep in myself I reached out like a drowning man and grabbed the lifeline. Without understanding the process, I began to let the principle of Cheng Man-ching's Tai Chi begin to dissolve my brittle but carefully constructed personality.

The next two years passed like a dream. I learned the Tai

Chi form and felt that for the first time since I was a child I was living vibrantly. My long-held wish that life would be a joyous adventure was coming true.

I stopped worrying about succeeding and fitting in. I let my hair grow long, quit my part-time job, stopped writing, and got a divorce. I threw myself into the anti-Vietnam War movement, discovered sexuality, became creative.

I took my inspiration from many sources—rock music, psychedelic drugs, hippies, leftists—but at the core was a little Chinese man who said, "Relax. Let go of all your tension. Relax completely."

The fifties had made it very hard, but the sixties made it too easy. To help make the war palatable to the American people, Lyndon Johnson promised them "guns and butter." In order to deliver on that promise, the government borrowed heavily against the treasury. Eventually the piper would be paid, but for a while the economy flourished. Lots of money was around to support frugal hippies who just needed a space to crash. Drugs were abundant and cheap. Sex required little or no responsibility.

There was a moral center to the counter-culture and anti-war movement—they represented great, positive change—but there was also flaccidity and self-indulgence.

I heard Professor Cheng when he said, "Relax." But it was only one half of a whole. The other half, to which I paid less attention, is the sense of discipline, integrity, and rootedness. Only when you are in balance can you relax and let go of the tension and hardness.

I had glimpsed the principle, which allowed me to embark upon my great adventure, but I lacked grounding and understanding in depth.

Forsaking the innocence and clarity that had launched me, I used my few years of martial arts training to erect a fantasy persona—the super-warrior.

There was a shot of me on TV at a demonstration, blocking a policeman's club and defying another on horseback. "Who is that guy?" people began to ask.

At another demonstration, a heckler tried to grab my beard. Six years had passed since the first incident, and I had learned a little something in the meantime. As he pulled, I pushed. He seemed to fall back an unbelievable distance; at fifty feet he was still stumbling backward in amazement, picking up speed as he went, his arms pinwheeling, his legs flying out.

Despite this thrilling first application of Tai Chi, my image as the anti-war movement "super-warrior" was mostly illusion, smoke, and mirrors. But in the army of the powerless, warriors were desperately sought. By the end of the sixties, I was near the forefront of the anti-war movement.

I believe it was Oscar Wilde who said, "There can be two tragedies in a person's life. One is that they never get what they want. The other is that they get it."

My myth was succeeding much too well, especially with the vast police establishment of the time. After all, considering the money and manpower they were expending, they needed an opponent of violence and aggression, not "flower power."

At the Democratic convention in Chicago in '68, in the control room of the government's massive police operation against the demonstrators, there was a chart listing the leaders of the enemy forces. And my name was at the top.

The event that most defined my myth to the police was

43

during the week prior to the convention when I "taught" Karate in the park, on national television, concentrating on techniques to assault policemen.

A month after the convention, the poet Allen Ginsberg, who later became a student of Cheng Man-ch'ing's Tai Chi Chuan, remonstrated with me. "You helped create a vibration of fear and violence. Why didn't you teach Tai Chi instead of Karate?"

"That's a very good question," I answered, still wearing the cast on my arm and stitches in my head from the severe beating I'd received at the end of the convention.

My personal descent into pain and paranoia was paralleled in the movement in which I was a part. The election of Richard Nixon, which my actions helped bring about, changed the game. No longer did we happily cry, "Make love, not war." The anti-war refrain became "Bring the war home."

It wasn't fun anymore. Though I still managed a couple of rounds of form a day, and even to occasionally attend class, I didn't have much time for Tai Chi. I had become a terrorist. Instead of "relaxation," my life turned into a desperate conspiracy. My new playthings were guns and dynamite.

Finally it became a constant nightmare. I awoke each night chilled, soaked in a pool of sweat. I felt guilty to be alive when others had been killed, and terrified of the knock at the door in the middle of the night that would mean I had been found out.

I went to Cheng Man-ch'ing for advice. I told him that I was involved in a dangerous enterprise that I no longer had the stomach for, but I felt I owed it to my friends not to abandon them.

"Leave that bad place," he said. "Don't go there anymore. And you don't need to worry about what people will think of you. Just leave it in my hands. Come here and learn Tai Chi."

Did he have a sense of what was going on in my world, or was it like his Push Hands—all he knew was where *my* energy wanted to go, and he was just helping me get there?

I was at a crossroads. If I continued on my present path, I felt I would be killed. If I withdrew from activism, entering Professor's monastery, as I thought of it in my mind, I would survive and perhaps someday become in reality the warrior that I was now only in fantasy.

Turning my back on my comrades and the war, I got a room and a part-time job, and became a dedicated student of Tai Chi Chuan. From 1970 through '75, I studied seriously with Professor, eventually becoming an assistant, and practiced Push Hands about six hours a day, seven days a week.

Overtly I wrestled with the secret of Professor's *gung fu*—what was it that made him so great at Tai Chi? How could I become like him? When he pushed it felt irresistible, as if a mountain range were moving through you. When you tried to push him it was like trying to push a summer breeze.

On a deeper level, I was trying to complete my lifelong quest for true power. I knew he had it. I kept waiting, watching, and listening for him to give up his secret.

I heard what I felt were clues—how for years he did push hands all day, until he was so tired that when he got home at night he collapsed, without the strength to put his feet on the bed. Nevertheless, everyone was able to push him around, until one night he dreamt that his arms had been cut off at

45

the shoulders. "From that day forward," he said, "no one could touch me."

Another story that resonated was about his being near death. "The doctors only gave me six months to live. Through the study of Tai Chi I cured my illness and regained my health. Since I thought I was going to die, now I feel that every day of these fifty years has been a gift." He seemed to live that way, as if he woke up each new day to the gift of life.

For all he stressed the importance of Tai Chi as a health exercise, all the time I studied with him I never really listened. I was young, and I thought I was in good health. All his chatter about health was a vague annoyance to me; it seemed that it distracted him from opening the secret door of his power.

Many years later, as my *ch'i* grew and my heart softened and healed, I began to understand that joyousness is simultaneously the primary cause and primary effect of great good health. I finally began to really hear his words.

> ... Let true affection and happy concourse abide in this hall. Let us here correct our past mistakes and lose preoccupation with self. With the constancy of the planets in their courses or of the dragon in his cloud-wrapped path, let us enter the land of health and ever after walk within its bounds. Let us fortify ourselves against weakness and learn to be self-reliant, without even a moment's lapse. Then our resolution will become the very air we breathe, the world we live in; then we will be as happy as a fish in crystal waters ...*

---

*From Professor's dedication to his school, "The Hall of Happiness."

You Must Love Yourselves

Professor described himself as being 70 percent Confucius and 30 percent Lao Tzu. The concept of *"ren,"* translated as humanism, loving kindness or love, is central to both Confucius and Professor Cheng's Tai Chi Chuan.

Once a group of us were hanging out in the front room at the original Tai Chi Association on Canal Street. Professor was preparing to leave the school. He had already put on his cloak when he was drawn into a political conversation with the students, in itself a rather unique occurrence.

Professor was a staunch anti-Communist. He had left his beloved China with Chiang Kai-shek's Kuomintang when they were defeated by the Communist armies under the leadership of Mao Tse-tung. It was a bitter exile in Taiwan for this quintessential Chinese man, though he made the most of it. He was a founding member of the Nationalist Assembly, a physician, painter—one of his students was Madame Chiang Kai-shek, who wrote the introduction to a book of his paintings—and, of course, he continued studying and teaching Tai Chi Chuan. (Chiang Kai-shek himself wrote an introduction to Professor's *Thirteen Treatises.*)

He had lost his homeland to the Communists, and the classical teaching and principles which were of unsurpassed importance to him were held to be reactionary and criminal by the Communist government.

There were few of us in the room during our "political discussion" who were at all sensitive to what Communism represented to him, but we blithely argued the then-fashionable pro-leftist, anti-Vietnam War position, which he alone in the room opposed. Being senior to the rest of the group, and with some experience in anti-war politics, I marveled at the clear, hearty, affectionate spirit he maintained. I had by that time participated in hundreds of similar "discussions," which were always charged with anger and defensiveness, as though losing the argument meant an invalidation of our positions and of ourselves, as if the outcome of the war itself depended on each side beating down the other in the "discussion."

But not this time. Smiling, without a trace of anger or defensiveness, he presented his argument, heard us out and then left, saying, "You have to learn to love yourselves."

How curious, I thought; at the the height of the raging Vietnam War, this old, dedicated anti-Communist telling a roomful of hippie leftists that we must "learn to love ourselves"?

Many years later, I found myself answering questions in a roomful of Tai Chi students. One asked, "Did you ever see Professor Cheng angry?" It suddenly struck me that in seven years I could only remember one time that he lost his temper.

It was at the school on Canal Street. I was in the main practice room one afternoon; Professor was in the front room meeting with a small group of the Chinese sponsors of the Tai Chi Association. Suddenly there was a loud crash in the front room.

I peeked in and saw Professor, his eyes blazing, standing at the table while everyone else sat frozen, pressed back against their chairs.

Tam, who was at the meeting, later told me what had happened. Professor announced that he was returning to Taiwan for a year. The sponsors then declared that the school would be off-limits to the non-Chinese students. Professor was so angered that he slammed his hand down on the table, ending the discussion.

It turned out to be a Pyrrhic victory. They wouldn't confront him directly, but once he had left for Taiwan the Chinese sponsors did lock the rest of us out of the school, and we had a difficult time finding new premises.

Although it surprised me at the time, it makes perfect sense that I can only remember that he lost his temper once. Anger is itself a fear reaction. It does not come from that core in us that connects to the divine. What Professor's *gung fu* was essentially about was relaxing fear—physical or psychological—and he had gotten very good at it.

Another questioner asked how Professor dealt with the political currents of the late sixties and early seventies. I remembered the "discussion" we had in his office, and the loving way in which he had related to us. It also reminded me of something an old political comrade had told me many years before, upon returning from a visit to Vietnam during the war.

"It's very interesting," he said, "but even though we're bombing and killing them, the Vietnamese seem not to hate the Americans. They're determined to defeat the government that's sending the soldiers, but they don't hate the

American people. They are actually a great deal gentler than we are," he said, referring to those of us in opposition to the war.

It was true that though we in the movement opposed the war—for many of us *all* war—there was actually little peace in our hearts. We hated the President and the government, we hated the military-industrial complex, and we hated the great "silent majority" of Americans who supported or acquiesced to the genocidal conflict. And, of course, we hated the police.

The worst part of hating is what it does to the hater. Generally, one's emotions reflect one's deepest sense of oneself. Probably we didn't think we were doing enough to stop the war. We had "dropped out" but we hadn't really dropped in. We were opposed, but we weren't in affirmation. We were angry, and on the deepest level anger is the armor that a fearful person wears to protect himself against his fear of who and what he really is.

How many of us on the left would destroy our lives because we were so desperately trying to deny the guilt we carried deep inside? It became so hard for us to love life, or to love another person, because we couldn't love ourselves.

The Air of Resiliency

"Breathe in the *ch'i* of heaven to become resilient as an infant," was Professor's basic advice for the study of Tai Chi Chuan. "In practicing Tai Chi," he said, "the breath should be long, thin, slow and quiet. In doing Push Hands, can you throttle your breath down so it's like a small child's?"

This is impossible to do if you're grunting and sweating, striving aggressively to overwhelm, or desperately trying to avoid defeat. Tension and hard force make the breath rough and choppy. The more you relax, the longer and finer the breath. Also, relaxation lets you deepen your breathing, allowing for a greater accumulation of air, the foundation for all *ch'i* development.

Professor taught that the best method was through what he called "listening." In Push Hands, listen to the center and energy of the opponent; in the form, listen to yourself, most fundamentally the breath.

Another of the ways Professor taught us to listen to ourselves was to be sensitive to perspiration. He would often say, "When you are sweating, it's no good; take a break." If he saw sweat breaking out on your forehead when you did Push Hands with him or were practicing alone, he would smile, point to the perspiration and direct you to take a seat.

"Sweating," he said, "is a sign that the *ch'i* is being dissipated. It comes from tension and it's as if you are depleting your bank account. Doing Tai Chi, you want to accumulate *ch'i*, not spend it. So, if you sweat, you should stop and rest.

"Actually, when you do Tai Chi, you shouldn't sweat. If you were meditating, would you perspire? The same should be true of Tai Chi Chuan."

The goal is the resilience of an infant's body—but we also seek the resilient mind.

It is something of a riddle why returning to the resilience of our infancy should be such a difficult matter.

Once Professor attended a private screening of a documentary by the filmmaker Robert Young, about a small group of Eskimos who were almost all that remained of their traditional culture. When the film was over, someone asked the old man if the Eskimos would be good at Tai Chi. "They don't need Tai Chi," he laughed. "They already have it. They are like bears, full of *ch'i*."

I suspect that the reason the rest of us need Tai Chi Chuan is that, as a result of our being socialized for this industrial age, we are alienated from and therefore feel guilty about our real selves. All our tightness is defense, erected to protect ourselves from who we really are.

To relax the breath and allow it to lead the *ch'i* to accumulate in the *tan tien*, we progressively relax past layers of physical and psychological armor. Finally relaxing the breath will allow it to confront and dissolve the deep guilt that blocks us from embracing our true nature.

This is the place where developing our *ch'i* becomes loving ourselves, which is the basis of all love.

Faith

Professor Cheng once offered a friendly criticism of his American students: "You are like bad card players," he said. "You let everybody see your cards. Being an honest person is not the same as letting everybody see your hand. You should learn to hold your cards close to yourself."

Through years of studying with Cheng Man-ch'ing, I came to be aware of many of his activities both within and outside the school: his painting and poetry, his study of the Chinese classics, his love of nature and of his family.

The more I knew about him, the stronger was my sense of how little I really knew who he was. There was an inaccessibility that had to do with a vast cultural distance between him and the rest of us—not just that he was Chinese, but that in many ways he was like someone out of a time machine.

Most of his students—indeed, the great majority of the society in which he found himself—were undergoing a crisis of the spirit. It has become a materialistic age. The same science that has produced our material progress is responsible for the death of the old beliefs. Our belief is in money, in mechanistic fury, in the ultimate lack of meaning. For all that we mouth traditional Judeo-Christian prayers, our real

faith—as we awaken to our day or descend into our night—
is in chaos.

The "Boxer Rebellion" in China at the turn of the cen-
tury was a crucial political event. The Boxers were mem-
bers of martial arts societies. People believed that they were
invulnerable to bullets. The Boxers led masses of Chinese
in human-wave assaults against the guns of Western troops.
They were slaughtered, and the rebellion was crushed.

Professor Cheng told us one day about the Boxers who
led this rebellion. "They had the faith of the people they
led," Professor said, "because they had demonstrated their
ability to withstand bullets. They would let a rifle be shot
at them, and the bullets would bounce off."

"The trouble was," Professor went on to say, "that these
Boxers could only do it if they were focusing their attention right at the gun. When the battle began, it was all the
rifles shooting at them from various angles that nullified
their power and killed them."

What kind of man believed this sort of stuff?

Describing his belief system, Professor would often refer
to the writing of Mencius, another exponent of Confucian-
ism.

Asked what he was good at, Mencius once replied, "I am
good at cultivating my flood-like *ch'i*. This is a *ch'i* which
is, in the highest degree, vast and unyielding. Nourish it
with integrity and place no obstacle in its path, and it will
fill the space between Heaven and Earth. It is a *ch'i* which
unites rightness and Tao. Deprive it of these and it will collapse."*

In his lecture on the "Three Fearlessnesses" Professor

Mencius, translated by D.C. Lau, Penguin Books 1970.

again quoted Mencius: "If the mountain of Tai should collapse in front of me, my face would not change countenance. It is because I have cultivated the greatness of my *ch'i*."

The understanding of "the greatness of the *ch'i*" is the core of Professor Cheng's spiritual belief.

✗ Where there is tension, the body is dead. Chi is the stuff of life. Let go of the body's stiffness and the *ch'i* flows; where the *ch'i* flows, what was stiff and dead becomes alive.

The same is true on the psychological plane. As Professor said, that which we seek to relax is fear. "The more we relax, the less we are afraid; the less we are afraid, the more we relax." This being the case, it is very important to understand that fear is not just that which we equate with terror. A car speeds around the corner as I am crossing the street, almost hitting me. For a split-second my heart is in my mouth; I am terrified.

Then the car passes. Enraged, I yell an obscenity at the driver. Surprised pedestrians look at me and I feel a sense of shame, that I'm making a fool of myself. As I continue down the street, I become depressed; I feel like killing the driver, but I can't do anything with my feeling but stew in it!

It's quite possible that I could spend the better part of a day flitting through a spectrum of unpleasant, painful, negative emotions having to do with this one incident—and never acknowledge that every one of those negative emotions was based in fear. Fear has ten thousand faces. Rage, guilt, depression—everything we feel as a state other than relaxation, happiness, and well-being—is a fear reaction.

Some might believe that we need our fear, that it's a necessary tool: "Your fear is what helped you jump out of the way of the car that almost hit you."

In fact it was my vitality, my *ch'i*, that got me out of the way of the car. All my fear did was cause a split-second of immobility that delayed my movement, that stiffened me and retarded the simple reflex response.

Let's take the example of Push Hands: Someone tries to push me; I am afraid, I stiffen up and get pushed. Again they try; this time I get angry, and I stiffen up and get pushed. Then I get depressed and gloomy, my mind wanders, and once again I get pushed. Three separate fear reactions prevent me from dealing with the push.

Eventually I may get it. The person tries to push me. I stay relaxed, sensitive, alive in the moment. There is no resistance or hard, tense force for his push to land on. He loses his balance, and since I have not leapt away fearfully, I am in position to send him flying.

Fear has no value. It is never necessary or helpful. It is bad for your *ch'i*, bad for your health, bad for your well-being. We first learn about the tension in body, shoulders, arms, and abdomen; we learn to relax and let it go. Then we learn about the tension in our mind. Its name is "fear."

Death and Dying

In the "Three Fearlessnesses" lecture, Professor Cheng quoted Lao Tzu about a child lying alone in the wilderness: "A rhinoceros's horn will not harm it. A tiger's claw will not tear it. A soldier's sharp weapons will have no place to land. It is because the baby has no concept of death."

"Can I concentrate my *ch'i* to become resilient?" Professor asks. "If a person is not resilient, he is hard and rigid. Therefore, to understand the principle of Tai Chi thoroughly, one must have the spirit of great fearlessness."

There was a fellow student who studied Tai Chi Chuan for a number of years and who worked as a tree surgeon. One day he fell from the top of a tree. It was a long fall, but all he suffered was a sprained wrist.

After the accident he told me he owed a great debt to Tai Chi Chuan. "Had that accident happened before I started studying," he said, "that fall would have hurt me very badly. As I was falling I just told myself, 'Relax.' I hit the ground soft, and it was amazing how easy I got off, considering the height."

The idea of "investing in loss" that Professor said was the key to learning Push Hands has deeper meaning than learning how to defeat an opponent.

Professor said, "If I have no body, how can any harm befall me? No matter how ferocious the weapons that oppose me, they are no threat." Better even than carrying the idea that I can defeat anyone is the idea that nothing can harm me.

If we can really invest in loss—not just as a technique, but to where it becomes part of our being—we can hit the wall with great force, we can fall, we can lose, and understand that if we don't resist we will not be hurt in any way.

The hurt and pain are not in birth, death, all our challenges and trials, but in our resistance to these events.

Just as it's necessary to understand the reality of fear, it's necessary to get beneath the illusion that material reality has power over us.

"Put your *ch'i* and heart-mind together in your *tan tien*." Professor said this was the central jewel of our Tai Chi, so important that "If you really practice this single idea, you don't have to do the rest of the *gung fu* of Tai Chi Chuan."

From the perspective of *ch'i*, the universe is like a mirror. It doesn't create reality and thrust it on us, but reflects our energy back upon us. We are the true creators of reality, not blind fate or chaos. Joyful, courageous persons will place themselves in a heavenly universe; depressed, fearful persons will shape a life that is hell.

Ch'i is like light to the darkness of our fear. All you have to do is turn on the light. The power to make miracles resides in understanding that the greatness of our *ch'i*, or lack of it, creates the universe.

There is an interesting passage at the end of Chapter 16 in the *Tao Te Ching*, which is commonly translated that the life of a Taoist will be preserved from harm. But Professor Cheng has a different, more mystical interpretation:

If in accord with the Tao, one is everlasting, "And even though his body ceases to be, he is not destroyed."*

Traditionally, Taoists—those "in accord with the *Tao*"—were called "immortals." Though Professor asserted on more than one occasion that he had "no wish to be an immortal, my only wish is to be a human being," he was also an excellent card player who held his cards close to his vest. Whether or not he was an "immortal," he resonated with a sense of "the greatness of the *ch'i*."

Does Professor's reference to immortality in the *Tao Te Ching* represent a philosophic premise, that one in accord with Tao lives on in memory, in the virtue of his life and works? Or does it refer to something else, a physical principle that can reveal itself in "the greatness of the *ch'i*," and represent a directive to reach out to a place in ourselves that is deathless?

---

*Lao-Tzu: "My Words Are Easy To Understand," translated by Tam Gibbs, North Atlantic Books.

The Three Treasures
of Cheng Man-ch'ing

When we say that we are students of Cheng Man-ch'ing's Yang-style Tai Chi Chuan, probably that which most characterizes it is Professor's sense of the central principle, relaxation. Most other systems of Tai Chi Chuan—in fact, most other systems of martial art—recognize the importance of the principle, but Cheng Man-ch'ing takes it further.

Others might say, "Sure, relaxation is fundamental, but you can't be totally relaxed. That wouldn't work. You have to combine relaxation with some force to create a functional art."

However, for Professor Cheng, all tension and hard force block the development of the *ch'i*, the power of Tai Chi Chuan, both as a health exercise and as a functional system of self defense. Over the years, on many occasions, I heard students asking him about martial or "*ch'i gung*" concepts they discovered elsewhere. If there was any forcing or hardness involved—and there often was—he warned against it: "Too strong, bad for the *ch'i*, not good for your health."

Once we have embraced the principle of total relaxation, the rest of the foundation of Professor Cheng's Tai Chi Chuan is in his "Three Treasures."

First of these "treasures" is the place at the top of the head which presses upward and from which you imagine yourself suspended from heaven. This refers to the fundamental principle of straightness, keeping the spine absolutely straight, and the body leaning neither forward or back, nor tilting side-to-side. It is the other side of the coin of relaxation, that which makes it possible to relax. If you are not straight, you must use tension to preserve your balance. If you are not relaxed and straight, the thoroughfares of the *ch'i* cannot be completely open, and your *ch'i* and health will suffer.

Second is the "Rushing Spring" or "Bubbling Well" point, the place in the center of the foot just behind the ball of the foot, down through which one channels the weight into the ground and up through which, eventually, one produces the internal power.

The second "treasure" has to do with root. It is the key to function, the secret of being unpushable without the use of resistance, as well as being the wellspring of the unique internal power of Tai Chi Chuan. This internal power is not a technique just anyone can use. It is the result of the self-transformation of the Tai Chi player who relaxes to become resilient as a small child and, as a result, manifests a different energy system.

The third "treasure" is the most important of all. Professor Cheng said, "The central idea in Tai Chi Chuan, the precious jewel of the discipline, is to put the *ch'i* and heart-mind together in the *tan tien*." This used to confuse me, because at other times he would say, "The central idea, the precious jewel, ... is to relax completely."

"Come on, now," I would say to myself, "Let's get it straight. Is the 'precious jewel' to relax, or is it to put the *ch'i* and heart-mind together in the *tan tien*?" Finally I came to realize that there was no contradiction; the essence of the principle of relaxation is in keeping the *ch'i* and heart-mind together in the *tan tien*. "Relaxation," and "*ch'i* and heart-mind together in the *tan tien*" is the same idea, the precious jewel of our Tai Chi Chuan.

The Three Points
in Push Hands

In Push Hands, one must be aware of three points. If you are in "Push," the three points are the opponent's elbow, wrist, and opposite elbow. You connect to their elbow and wrist with your two hands, and to their opposite elbow with your elbow. If you are in "Ward-off," the opposite is true but the points are the same.

You must be in contact with these three points as well as being sensitive to the opponent's energy through each one of them. This basic meeting place in Push Hands, with one player in Push and the other in Ward-off, is ideally a balanced, two-person shape. If one of the two players abandons the integrity of this shape, the other cannot maintain it alone. They must then understand what to do with the "broken" shape. The best way to achieve that "understanding" is to become deeply familiar with the correct shape.

The three points provide a protective frame for the players as they sense and take advantage of the opponent's excess or insufficiency. For the player in Push, having her hands on the opponent's Ward-off elbow and wrist is her protection against his striking out with his Ward-off arm. The position will enable her to draw him forward as he tries to push—or strike—and he will be completely off-balance and at her mercy. As a matter of fact, it provides similar protection should he try to attack with his other hand.

It is important that her hands be at the point of his wrist and elbow. If she is slightly off the wrist, his hand will be able to slide off and attack her body. Not being at the elbow denies her control of his arm. One of the greatest lessons of Push Hands, both as an exercise and as it translates into a more dangerous self-defense situation, is the value of developing an instinctive connection to the opponent's joints, especially the wrist and elbow. Connecting to these joints is a key to being able to control an opponent's energy with only a little force on your part, even when your opponent is very powerful.

Returning to the imagined player in Push—she has connected her hands to her opponent's Ward-off elbow and wrist. The third point is the opponent's opposite elbow, which she must connect to her own elbow. This provides protection if the opponent tries to strike her.

Professor Cheng described this third point, with the two elbows in contact, as being the cornerstone of "understanding" the Push Hands exercise. It acts as the fulcrum of a lever, providing what he called "control of the counter-balance."

Many players, after reaching a significant level of softness and sensitivity, are still frustrated by their inability to deal with much less advanced players. Part of the problem is in their lack of understanding of the "counter-balance"; they are not sticking to the opponent's elbow, so that when they turn to evade, nothing happens to the opponent. Neutralizing is not just escaping; it is simultaneously returning energy as you escape, like a revolving door, simultaneously emptying out one side as the other side fills up.

Another principle of Push Hands is that your energy should be neutral except when you release force at the opponent's stuckness. The postures of Ward-off, Rollback, and even Push and Press should be totally without force. You should be receptive, listening.

In doing Push Hands, "Push" should not push, she should listen, and if the opponent retreats she should follow; but if the opponent attacks, "Push" should become yielding, receiving his energy and drawing him off-balance. The same is true of the other three positions in "Grasping the Sparrow's Tail."

Returning to our hypothetical point of address, with one player in Push and the other in Ward-off—just as the "Pusher" needs to connect her hands to the opponent's elbow and wrist, the "Ward-off" player needs his elbow and wrist connected to his opponent's hands. Just as she is following his two points, so must he follow hers. Should her hands break contact with his elbow and wrist, he is vulnerable to where her hands might go. Again, in terms of the integrity of the two-person form of Push Hands, she has "broken" the connection, so he must react appropriately.

Just as she should have been listening to his center through his wrist and elbow, so should he be listening to her center through her two hands. Therefore, when she takes her hands away, whatever her intention, he should be able to instantly fill up the vacuum and push her center.

Understanding the form and its "Three Points" allows the Push Hands player to demystify energy. A beginning student looks at Push Hands and asks, "Yeah, but in a fight a whole lot of stuff is going on, fast and wild. How can this quiet little exercise do a damn thing in a situation like that?"

Later on, if they practice well, they begin to realize that the "whole lot of stuff happening" is still only happening one moment at a time. One piece of "stuff" is all that can happen at any one moment.

Push Hands training is to enable you to "understand" that *one* moment. If you really understand it, you don't need to worry about "all the other stuff that will follow."

Two beginners stand connected; she's in Push, he's in Ward-off. They are playing the game. Suddenly she takes her hands off his wrist and elbow and pushes at his chest. It happens in an instant and he stands there in Ward-off, totally at a loss. He must not lose faith and abandon form and principle, allowing the play to degenerate to wild shoving and blocking. He must study that first moment when she released from her connection to his Ward-off, until he can take advantage of the opening her disconnection gave him. Even if it takes him years of practice and study, he must understand that one piece of time.

Listening through the three points gives the player the chance to follow the opponent with the technique of triangulation, the best method of following. If he is chasing his opponent with just one point, it is relatively easy for her to turn him off. If he follows with two of the points, he can "triangulate" on her center and it will be a great deal harder for her to get away. Not only is triangulating the best way to get the opponent stuck, but Professor also called it the "fiercest" method of pushing, using both hands from two points, triangulating on the center. Done well, it will produce a thunderous meeting of the opponent's back with the wall.

The Three Pushes

Professor said that one of the keys to developing skill in Push Hands is differentiating the roles of "Pusher" and "Neutralizer." It is a great help in taking the quality of competitiveness—the "fight or flight" energy that blocks the *ch'i*—out of the play, and enables one to concentrate on pushing or neutralizing within the principle of "don't resist, don't insist." "If you are doing push hands with the idea of trying to push or not be pushed, it is not Tai Chi," said the old man.

The correct method is for the person with their back to the wall to focus entirely on neutralizing the pushes of the person facing the wall. After a while, they reverse positions and take the opposite roles.

The Neutralizer must be able to deal with a sequence of three potential pushes: Push, Press, and Shoulder Strike. He must be able to turn off the first two and still have room left to deal with his opponent's last resort, the shoulder. The Pusher, for her part, must know her limit and not lunge forward. The position requiring the most work is the last, especially for the person practicing neutralizing. There is where he must learn the substantiality of the insubstantial.

In Push Hands, a mark of the beginner is great confidence in front-leg positions and an equal lack of confidence in having the weight on the rear leg. But the principle of Push Hands is that you must give the opponent whatever he wants; you must not block his energy. "What he wants" for most opponents will be the "confidence" of the seemingly more stable, powerful front-leg positions, so you must be able to handle them from your back leg. Professor used to laugh and hit his two fists together as two bullish players attacked each other leaning front leg to front leg, like rams butting horns.

"The posture," he said, "which most epitomizes Tai Chi Chuan is Rollback, in which you don't resist your opponent but let him push in as far as he wants. Then, when he has come in too far, you throw him off. It is called 'setting a trap.'"

When you are confident about 'setting a trap,' when you have developed the root and technique of the rear-leg positions, you will be able to neutralize and be a true Tai Chi player.

The Three Gates

Central to the technique of neutralizing is what Professor called "folding." He said, "Folding is the secret of how you can use softness in Push Hands to defeat strong, aggressive people." To understand "folding" you must know about the "Three Gates." The first is the gate of the shoulder; the second is the gate of the waist; and the third is the gate of the ankle. The technique of folding is to open the first two gates, one after the other; ideally the third should never be opened.

Imagine a "strong, aggressive person" who pushes you. He lunges forward with his arms and his body. At the end of his push he has reached the limit of his balance in his forward position. At this point, in trying to deal with this kind of push, a beginner will usually find herself tottering at the limits of her rear leg, if she has managed to survive the push at all.

When an aggressive person reaches the end of his attack and has not succeeded, it is a place of danger and opportunity because he is likely to desperately keep attacking beyond his place of balance. In the situation we have just described, with both players at the limit of their postures, as he continues forward in some crude, off-balance push, she is also likely to be defeated.

"Folding" allows the player in the neutralizing mode to in effect assimilate the attacker's range of movement without sacrificing very much of her own.

Think of an attack as having a potential range of movement, from rear to front, of 100 percent. Anything beyond that is off-balance. The Neutralizer has a similar range, from front to rear, of 100 percent. By allowing her arm to fold in from the shoulder, and skillfully turning her waist as her opponent attacks, the Neutralizer can "eat up" the full 100 percent of his attack while only sacrificing a small percentage of her own. In Professor's words, he has depleted his bank account while she still has a lot left in her own. At this point she has opened the "gate of the shoulder."

Then, as desperation takes hold in him, as it likely will, and he lunges in an off-balance attack, she has 80 percent or so left to deal with his suicidal behavior. She will then have a much easier time dealing with his lunge than she would if she were desperately hanging on to her last bit of leg in her rear position. As he lunges, she withdraws, using as much of her 80 percent as she needs. Since he was already at his limit, it will probably not be much. This withdrawal is "opening the gate of the waist."

Being pushed is having the gate of the ankle opened. Good folding technique should prevent you from being pushed, so this third gate need never be opened.

Folding can also be used in following and attacking. It's clearest in a Ward-off attack: triangulate on the opponent's center through his hands. If he presses in or is hard at one point, yield there but fill up the weakness he has developed at the other point. A quality of Tai Chi—empty and full—is that hardness always creates a counter-line of weakness; folding allows you to follow the two points until the opponent ends up stuck, with no place to go. Then you release your energy, "triangulating" for utmost "ferocity" of attack.

The Bow

In the popular Wilhelm/Baynes translation of the *I-Ching*, or *Book of Changes*, one of the great classics of Chinese philosophy, there is the following footnote to the hexagram "Modesty":

> There are not many hexagrams in the *Book of Changes* in which all the lines have an exclusively favorable meaning, as in the hexagram of Modesty. This shows how great a value Chinese wisdom places on this virtue.*

One day Professor Cheng made an announcement that caused some disturbance at the school. He said that to begin the new series of lectures on Confucius, there would be a ceremony during which all the students would kowtow to a picture of Confucius, a formal ceremony consisting of kneeling, bowing the head to the floor three times, standing, kneeling again until a total of three kneelings and nine bowings was completed.

The idea appealed to some and embarrassed others while a few—an old friend of mine among them—had deep reservations. For a religious Jew this ceremony reeked of the

---

*_I-Ching_, Wilhelm/Baynes, Pantheon Books.

"Worshipping of Graven Images" forbidden in the Ten Commandments. My friend found it so upsetting that he quit the study of Tai Chi.

After some politicking by Professor's assistants, assuring the students that to the Chinese "kowtowing" is simply a traditional statement of respect without the Western connotations of worship, the ceremony took place. Professor chanted a poem in Chinese in honor of the event. Then the student body, minus a few diehards, knelt and performed the ceremony.

It was short and pleasant, and Professor was pleased, though he later joked that kowtowing was difficult for Westerners: "You try to humble yourselves with your forehead to the floor, but your ass sticks up in the air arrogantly."

Bob Smith writes of how, when he first wanted to study with Professor Cheng in Taiwan, he started giving him gifts. Professor took the gifts but did not accept Bob as a student. Finally he sent Bob to study with one of his senior students. Only after a year was Bob able to study with Professor Cheng himself.

One of the ways Professor Cheng had compromised his teaching for his American students was to eliminate the traditional bowing to the teacher in becoming a formal disciple. However, although it was modified, the principle of respect from student to teacher as well as the principle of respect itself was not modified. It was central to the *Tao* he taught.

A common misunderstanding among students of Tai Chi is that the exercise and philosophy exist separately. This misunderstanding is based on the Western attitude that philosophy is abstract and metaphysical. Generally, the Chinese have a different sense, viewing philosophy as the underpin-nings of their arts and sciences. To think of Tai Chi as exist-ing apart from Taoist and Confucian philosophy is like looking at an automobile separate from its engine. Tai Chi existing without its philosophical foundation would become a hollow form of adult exercise, lacking not only the pro-fundity of the art but its great health and martial arts bene-fits as well.

One of the exercises that supplements our basic Tai Chi is the *"Da Liu"* exercise, a two-person form that deals with the martial application of a handful of postures. The *Da Liu*, as would a formal round of Push Hands, begins with a bow. There is a tradition in our Tai Chi that the most impor-tant comes first—true of the form, for instance, and true of the *Da Liu*.

This gesture of respect for the opponent is functional, not simply ritual. The art of Tai Chi does not work if the opponent has been demonized. A demonized opponent implies a condition of fear, and where fear is present the *ch'i* is blocked. It is not an empty spiritual statement to say that "one must love one's opponent." If your energy toward your opponent is not soft, is not "play," you had better call a cab in a hurry, because your Tai Chi will not work.

This is not to say that one should give oneself up when one bows. Professor said of the *Da Liu* bow, "I always incline slightly less than my opponent."

Bow modestly, but be completely aware. Should an ag-gressive, greedy person spring at you in the middle of your bow, he should be surprised, not you.

The bow in *Da Liu* has additional value. A paradox of the "greatness of the *ch'i*" is that it often exists more in its smallness than its vastness. Egotism and arrogance are weak because they are too expansive. Trying to take too much, one loses everything.

"Putting the *ch'i* in the *tan tien*," the central idea of Tai Chi, has the implication of "concentration." Make the *ch'i* firm and powerful by concentrating it in the *tan tien*, as you would take loose snow and compress it in your hands to make a snowball. Gradually this core of concentrated energy increases, becoming greater and greater, preserving its quality of concentrated power as it grows.

If, out of ambition or greed, you try to take on too much, allowing your will to take over and using your internal, real power to go after material things—wealth, status, power over others—you will discover that you have dissipated that internal power, even though you may have gained the external power of "things."

In order to develop the greatness of the *ch'i*, one needs to be humble. Lao Tzu says, "Gentle the will (in order to) strengthen the bones." Willfulness, the quality of ego and arrogance, weakens the kidneys, the seat of *ch'i* development. Subdue willfulness and you strengthen the uro-genital system and the entire process of nurturing the *ch'i*. You gain internal power as well as the "strengthening of the bones," where the *ch'i* overflows from the *tan tien* and enters the marrow. This makes the bones like steel and not only retards the so-called "normal" processes of aging—the bones becoming brittle—but even reverses it. This reversal of the aging process is the reason why Tai Chi is so popular in China, and according to Professor Cheng is the most important reason to study the art.

The bow should be an assertion of who and what you really are. Not what you have in your pocket, in your bank account; not what the world says about you, the neighborhood you live in, or the college from which you graduated. What you really are is a core of energy that connects you to the cosmos and grows in power as you remain consistent with it.

I suspect that this is what Jesus meant when He said, "The meek shall inherit the earth." "Meekness" is a perhaps unfortunate way of describing "humility." What humility offers the individual is the opportunity to concentrate and harness the real power of the universe. That is the only power with the greatness to "inherit the earth."

The Indian greeting, "*Namaste*," "the divinity in me salutes the divinity in you," expresses the proper attitude of a Tai Chi player. It is this attitude that subdues your fearful need to dominate. It allows you to accept the essential interconnection of yourself and your opponent, let go of your demons, and relax into the concentrated greatness of your *ch'i*.

A Spiritual Discipline

A literal meaning of the words *Tao Te Ching,* the title of the text that is the basis of Tai Chi Chuan is that *"Tao"* is the supreme or divine principle and *"Te"* is the conduct that expresses that principle. *"Ching"* means "book," so, taken together, *"Tao Te Ching"* means "the book about the supreme principle, and how one should live relative to it."

The study of Tai Chi Chuan may not qualify as religious training, but the study of our Tai Chi Chuan is—as Professor said—most fundamentally the study of *Tao.*

Lao Tzu said, "I can't begin to define this *Tao;* it's beyond my or anybody else's capacity to define. However, if you pressed me for a term, something to call it, I would call it 'mother.'"

Though *Tao* is too vast and wonderful for us to define, its feminine character is the key to *Te,* the mode of conduct based on *Tao.* Through the study of Tai Chi one becomes more receptive and sensitive, essentially softer. This softness is the bottom line expression of the *Tao* in the way we live.

It's been said that the reason women in our society are more sensitive than men is that they are less powerful; rather than overpowering people or situations, they are forced to be yielding, more sensitive to the moment, to try to find the path of least resistance, to use subtlety and wiles to affect a situation without directly confronting opposing force.

In Tai Chi Chuan we develop this mode of behavior not due to an underlying powerlessness, but rather the opposite. Professor Cheng once said, "Never underestimate the importance of being sensitive, even at the most superficial level, at the level of your skin." Whether your skin is hot or cold, or develops inflammation, irritation, or discoloration, it is a principle of health to be conscious of the perimeter of your energy field, so you'll be able to react appropriately before the problem grows deeper.

We should take care of our skin—not bump into things or let it get dried out by the sun. When we nurture *ch'i,* the skin should become as soft as a baby's.

Similarly, we have to protect the perimeter of our psychological energy field. As Lao Tzu said, followers of the *Tao* have their "yes" and their "no." It does not serve to deny your feelings, even if you realize that your anger or hurt is inconsistent with true principle. There are those who, "forsaking the near to seek the far," become like bad actors with false smiles, pretending they have mastered the emotions that are actually eating away at them.

You can't deny your feelings and also be sensitive to energy. If someone tries to push you, you can't just stand there pretending you didn't feel it, or that it didn't happen.

Gradually, paying close attention to energy over months and years, you soften in your response and learn to deal appropriately with another's hardness.

Most spiritual disciplines avow loving behavior, but the problem remains: How do you get there? How do you really make the "Golden Mean" a part of yourself, "not doing to another what you would not have them do to you?"

How many times has a follower of a spiritual discipline left his temple or monastery determined to act lovingly in the world, in the "marketplace," only to see that determination shatter in the face of the mundane world's coldness and cruelty?

Our *Chuan* (martial art) is a marvelous path to the Path, a *tao* leading us to *Tao*. First of all, it's necessary to understand that the only real opponent exists inside of each of us. We are all a battleground between truth and illusion, between faith in the supreme principle and faith in chaos.

The *Chuan* provides us with a superb judge in the crucial debate between your heart, which is in the company of *Tao*, and your programmed mind, which is the representative of chaotic materialism. Your heart says, "The way to live your life, the reflection of the *Tao*, is to be soft, tender, and peaceful."

Your mind puts forth a counter-argument: "Softness, tenderness, and peace are a fool's game. If you want to make your way in the world, you must be hard. The world is a cold, cruel place, so you must look out for 'Number One'; kill or be killed."

Chuan sits in judgement. It decides that it is hardness that is the fool's game. It proves to you that if you really want to make your way in the world, softness, tenderness, and peace are the best way.

It provides real, not abstract, proof: If a powerful, aggressive person rushes at you, determined to push you through the wall, and you offer him hardness, bad stuff is likely to happen to you. But if you can present the power of the soft, he will go flying and you will be untouched.

The *Chuan* says, "Don't even bother philosophizing about the relative virtue of softness versus hardness. I can show

79

you on the most fundamental level that softness works better. And if it works in the face of a violent attacker, how can you doubt its function in a relationship, or in the spirit with which you address each day's actions?" A final and even more compelling argument is the way the health of your skin, body, and cells will respond to the softness of your energy, as you can see hardness produce withering and death in those who don't understand.

The *Chuan* teaches us how the *Tao* functions. First of all, we must give up our need to control and manipulate. There is no posture in the form that is about either blocking or grabbing. As you play the form and imagine the applications, be aware that there are no "blocks"; we never oppose force with force. Rather, we use "four ounces to deflect a thousand pounds."

Similarly, grabbing is the kind of energy that is opposite to and blocks the *ch'i*, so no posture is a "grab." As a matter of fact, the thumb is connected in Taoist physiology to that very quality of willfulness that in excess depletes the energy of the uro-genital system, from where the *ch'i* grows. A footnote in the *Old Testament* might read that the use of the thumb—grabbing—is what got us kicked out of the Garden of Eden.

Lack of faith in principle forces one to put all one's faith in materialism. In Shakespeare's play *Othello*, the villainous Iago espouses materialistic philosophy, saying, "Put money in thy purse!" Iago has no faith in goodness or love, so he must look for his sole comfort in money, in the power of "things." Later in the play, Othello falls into the same trap when he accepts the evidence of a mere handkerchief—blatant material reality—as being more important than the love between Desdemona and himself.

It is both Shakespeare's and Professor Cheng's understanding that to choose materialism, a life of grabbing after things, over Supreme Principle is to doom oneself physically and spiritually.

Incidentally, beware in Push Hands of the tendency to grab your opponent as they push you. Grabbing will pull their energy toward you and, if they are skillful, the way you are increasing their power by adding your own can cause you great harm. By the same token, if you are in the position of being grabbed, don't resist, but allow that energy to add to your own. Being soft at the exact point of being grabbed—how you react in that first split-second—is a significant signpost on the road of the development of your Tai Chi Chuan. Even if you resist just slightly when first you are grabbed, and then go with the force, the power of the application will be almost entirely lost by that slight initial resistance.

In Push Hands, rather than oppose the opponent's energy, yield to him, "giving him what he wants." On the psychological level, fear operates as a need to be always in control, of not trusting in the flow of events. It's a fundamental tightness that blocks the benefit of the *ch'i* in our bodies and in our lives. We must give up our need to control in order to experience fullness, health, and joy. Tai Chi doesn't just preach that truth, it gives us a living experience of it.

Balance and Responsibility

Professor said that the behavior that leads to happiness is moderation—being in balance, neither excessive nor insufficient.

Half of the form's focus is on balance: the spine held straight, the sacrum hanging plumb, the body held as if suspended from heaven, neither leaning nor tilting. The other half of the focus is on relaxation; but without straightness, the body being in balance, you cannot relax. In the 70–30 percent postures the knee must not go over the toe, and the center of the soles of both feet must relax into the ground. Otherwise your posture will lack stability, and you will be off balance and tense.

Your energy must also be contained. In the form, study the perimeter formed by Ward-off. If correct, it is neither excessive nor insufficient; it will not have you overextend into the other person's space nor collapse your own.

The basic idea of Push Hands is to preserve one's balance in the face of attack. It is not that you are trying to push the other person, but rather if they try to attack, you will not have to relinquish your balance because of them. You are grounded and straight. If they try to penetrate to your left, you yield at your left, and fill up their emptiness from your right. The effect will be that they will be thrown as a result of their own behavior and you will have retained your balance.

The responsibility you have for your own balance is another great lesson Tai Chi teaches about how to live. You get first-hand that you are 100 percent responsible; the other person has nothing to do with it. Their push can be hard or soft, with a long or short energy burst, light or with great force; but whether or not you get pushed is not in their power. And neither is it their fault. You have the power over your own balance, no matter what they do.

In this historical period, Tai Chi's lesson of personal responsibility has tremendous importance. Whatever abuse or oppression we may experience, its effect on our balance is still in our hands. The excuse that a wrong suffered in the world must produce wrongful behavior in the individual is entirely that—an excuse.

Heart-Mind

The precious jewel that exists at the heart of our Tai Chi is in the phrase, "Let the *ch'i* and heart-mind mutually guard one another in the *tan tien*." The rest of the Tai Chi, in fact, is a playground where students can work with an endless series of ideas, without getting bored, but each one of those ten thousand ideas has at its core the idea of "putting the *ch'i* and heart-mind to guard one another in the *tan tien*."

Modern brain research has established the existence of two general qualities of consciousness, corresponding to the two hemispheres of the brain: so-called "left-brain" and "right-brain" thought. The left brain has to do with management, facts, and figures. It's what we use to work a crossword puzzle or study a contract. The right brain is intuitive and creative. It serves the artist in all of us.

Predating this research by millennia, the Chinese described two qualities of consciousness. The character for the "facts and figures" mind is different than for the "heart-mind," which is so important in Tai Chi.

The left brain manages our affairs in the world. It creates the ego, defines the individual as a unique entity. The right brain, the heart-mind, has the opposite influence, unifying rather than separating; it exists in the great unifying sea of the cosmos, the one that contains all.

Ideally, the two qualities of consciousness should be in balance. In our society we encounter the problem of the left-brain having almost totally suppressed the heart-mind.

We pay a great price for the suppression of the heart-mind because its power is limitless. It has the capacity to move and expand the *ch'i*, leading us to the "gateway to the miraculous."

It is a misunderstanding of the nature of the heart-mind when some "New Age" guru advises you to "listen to your heart" in order to find the answer to a complicated political question. The answers to those kinds of questions don't reside in the heart. The heart-mind basically knows just one thing—the greatness of the *ch'i*. If you know how to listen, it can tell you whether you're one with the flow of the *Tao* or blocked from it.

Basically, you can either feel a sense of clarity and joy— or its absence, characterized by tension, uptightness and the "ten thousand faces of fear."

What the heart cannot tell you is whether or not, for example, to support an increase in the income-tax deduction for dependent children. As a matter of fact, one of the reasons for the imbalance in the relationship of the ego-mind to the heart-mind is that the ego fears that its individuality will be destroyed—drowned in the "unifying sea of the cosmos"—by the heart-mind, so it tries to defend itself by blocking out its partner. But this is a false fear. The heart-mind has one job to do, and the ego has another.

For all the power of the heart-mind, one small point that takes on enormous weight is that of choice. What is responsible for whether we decide in this next moment to practice Tai Chi Chuan or watch television? To create or to stagnate? Choice is the province of the left brain, the ego-mind. The heart-mind practices non-action. It does not make choices; it does not buy and sell.

The voice of the heart is silent in the state of fear, but also in the state of diminished vitality. When our internal vitality is weakened, whether through sickness, immoderate habits, or excessive will, we lose awareness of our connection to the greatness of the *ch'i*, to the One. We will feel deeply tired, with no sense of our true power.

We may profess belief in the Supreme Principle, but it will be abstract and non-visceral. Beneath our outward "profession" of faith, our weakness will carry us to faithlessness, to the acquisition of material wealth, to dominance over others, to "the *gung fu* of death."

One of the greatest health benefits of Tai Chi Chuan is that it enables us to hear and heed the voice of our heart.

Professor Cheng in a characteristic mood.

A painting by Cheng Man-ch'ing.

Pointing to the character for "human." The symbol is of a man bowing.

Professor loved to fence, and it was the least formal class.

Sword form: "Parting the Grass in Search of the Snake."

"The Minor Literary Star."

Leading a form class: "Fair Lady Weaving at the Shuttle."

Demonstrating "Beautiful Lady's Hand," wrist and hand gently rounded, without any tension or hard force.

Another aspect of "Beautiful Lady's Hand," wrist loose like a whip ready to be cracked.

Professor talking about one of his many categories of "three."

Going home after a day's work.

Sticking

Recently I had a chance to play Push Hands with a student of the late Patrick Watson. This student had good grounding in the fundamentals, excellent posture, root, and grasp of the form. His deficiency was in his sticking, which can only be dealt with by time and practice. The ability to understand "sticking" is not only the essence of Push Hands but the key to Tai Chi as a martial art.

It brought back memories of my Tai Chi brother Patrick. When he first came to the Shr Jung school in New York, Pat was not very warmly received by the senior students at the school. He had studied Tai Chi as long as anyone, in addition to having an extensive prior martial arts background. But, as it was said at the time, he had a "real attitude." He was not going to be deferential in finding his place. "I may be from California," his manner boasted, "but I'm better than the best of you, and you're going to learn to like it."

Few did, though he was much beloved by Professor's assistant, Tam Gibbs, and a special favorite of Professor himself, who always had a soft spot in his heart for someone of real martial proficiency.

One day there was an election at the school. Professor

was establishing a directorate, a structure to maintain operations at the school in his absence.

The directors would be a few senior students appointed by the old man, but in deference to democratic principles he also wanted a group of six to be elected by the student body. A slate of candidates was proposed, and Pat was one of them. The election took place by secret ballot, and when the results had been tallied, Pat was not one of the six elected.

Professor stepped forward and spoke glowingly of Patrick Watson, then announced that we should recast our ballots, taking to heart what he had said about Pat.

So we voted again, and so great was the general antipathy that even with Professor's dramatic support, Patrick was again defeated. I don't believe I remember another occasion when Professor's wishes were defied so forcefully.

Undaunted, smiling with the usual twinkle in his eye, Professor announced, "This has been a very good election. Students have done very well. Now what we are going to do to make it even better is take the top five candidates who have just been elected, and in addition I will appoint Patrick Watson to help run the school."

If it occurred to the old man that he had not exactly followed democratic procedure, he didn't let on; he acted as if this were quite the natural and helpful thing to do.

Not surprisingly, Pat was still treated as an outsider by most of the students. Against my natural inclination, I decided to try to make him feel more welcome, so one night I invited him out to dinner. As was the general custom, I brought along a bottle of whiskey and poured us a drink.

Patrick smiled graciously and then poured the drink into his soupy rice. I refilled his glass, and he poured that into his congee. I persevered, and just as stubbornly he poured the drink into his congee. Finally my friend Nancy interceded, "Can't you see he doesn't want to drink?"

"What do you mean he doesn't want to drink?" I said. "Isn't he a student of Cheng Man-ch'ing?"

It turned out that he was. Not only did he continue to develop his own *gung fu* but he formed a large network of schools that spread Professor Cheng's Tai Chi Chuan all over the world.

In the last year of his life he invited me to speak to an assembly of his teaching assistants, close to a hundred people. I hadn't seen him in a number of years. I'd heard he'd been very sick, had suffered kidney failure and a number of heart attacks, and had undergone a tracheotomy that made our phone conversation difficult. When I got to the school, Pat hadn't yet arrived. He had requested that I wait in the anteroom so he could personally lead me in and introduce me to his teachers.

After sitting there for a while, I noticed an emaciated old man coming toward me. For a second I thought it was the janitor, and then I realized it was all that was left of huge, robust Patrick Watson.

He greeted me and took my arm to lead me into the main room. I was choked up until I felt an old feeling: Pat might have been one step away from the grave, but he had not lost his *gung fu*. Rather than leaning on me for support, he was up to his old tricks; he was sticking to my center, ever so subtly penetrating and controlling my balance point. He could hardly walk, and yet there he was, with me floating on his arm like a balloon on a string. It occurred to me that Tai Chi players never die, they just stick away.

Developing that level of skill requires a certain approach to Push Hands. The problem many students have, especially if they adopt a competitive attitude, is that they generalize their approach to energy. In other words, they hear their opponent's energy statement, but rather than carefully attend to the precise direction and reach of that energy—its exact quality—they in effect say to themselves, "Oh, here comes something toward my left side. I'm not going to worry about softness and sensitivity. I'll just give a rough tug and push them." Being more concerned with winning than with listening, they don't allow themselves to deepen their ability to sense ever more precise qualities of direction, force, and range.

We must not be satisfied to be dealing with the opponent's energy with 90 percent accuracy. In principle, this is 100 percent wrong. We must seek to be completely attuned to the precise quality of the opponent's energy. The method is to concentrate on sticking, putting the priority on "listening" rather than on winning or losing. Don't depend on force or speed. If the opponent moves quickly, you move quickly; if the opponent moves slowly, so should you.

The challenge is greater when a student begins to develop some ability. The temptation is to "cash in one's chips," using sensitivity to set off a crude, generalized response to the clues one's been given. The result is many victories, but little real progress.

The correct *gung fu* is like making a fine sword. We have the principle of self-awareness and softness; then we use Push Hands to temper that principle over and over again in the white-hot fire of our ego and fear, fueled by our opponent's ego and fear. What we emerge with is not a principle that we can only contact in a protected, meditative environment, but one steeled in the cauldron of negative emotions. Therefore we can use it at the most challenging moments of our lives.

The place in our Push Hands that represents the greatest challenge is when we put our backs to the wall and work on neutralizing. Professor said that neutralizing is ten times more difficult than pushing, so taking the position of the neutralizer pretty well guarantees that at least your ego will take a beating, if not your back.

You will be able to respond to the majority of attacks by using Rollback, especially playing against a novice. With a more skilled opponent, you are likely to have to confront what Professor termed "the most difficult attack of all: the *Yin*, feminine attack that goes across your body, opposite the expectation of Rollback.

"It's the most difficult attack to escape," he added, "because it is the attack that gives you the least amount of time to react."

To deal with this "most difficult attack" you have to know how to "Wipe." The clearest example of Wiping in the form comes just after the posture "Punch" in the first half. Wiping is itself the essence of neutralizing: the opponent pushes forcefully but you are not there; then you add to their force in the direction it's going and, depending on how much force they are exerting, they can be thrown a great distance.

When you do Rollback in the face of an attack, you have a wide range of motion in the waist; but when the attack goes in the other direction, across your body, the waist is much more limited in its movement and you can quickly get stuck. The Wipe must therefore be a solid part of your Push Hands repertoire or you will be in effect a one-sided player, crippled by your need to always force the opponent's energy to your Rollback. If you can only think in one direction, you can't be loose.

The technique of the Wipe has something of the magician's sleight of hand about it; it's a kind of energy illusion.

Using the example of the Punch posture: The opponent takes your right elbow in his left hand, your right wrist in his right, and attempts to draw them across your body. If he succeeds in locking either your shoulder or your hip, you will be lost. You start to turn your waist in the direction he is pulling you, but you can only go so far. In order to avoid getting stuck you place your left hand by your right elbow, just in back of his left hand.

Now comes the "sleight of hand." You free yourself by turning your waist back again, replacing your right elbow with your left hand. In order to preserve the illusion, it is crucial that you not use any force with your left hand. You don't force him off your elbow—that would give the whole thing away.

What you need to do is to place your hand behind his and take your elbow away. He will in that split-second be unaware on the level of his energy that you have traded your hand for your elbow. If you have done it correctly, he will not realize that he no longer has your arm! Depending on the force of his attack, he will continue for a short or long time in his intended direction, before he realizes that he has been tricked. But it will be too late; as is indicated by the sequence in the Form after the Punch, you will be in a great position to use Push and send him flying.

Although this is a complicated procedure to describe, it is actually quite simple but not easy. If you are to be successful, it must happen quickly, both to preserve the "illusion" and because you have so little time.

To complicate matters further, from the point of view of

our imaginary *"Yin"* attacker, his objective would be to attack in such a way as to make your Wipe impossible.

He would do this by attacking your elbow without giving you the option of either Rollback or Wipe. He would attempt to stick to your elbow, following you without declaring his energy in either of the two directions you need to get him off your center. If you cannot hear him, he will follow you until you are stuck and then release his energy and push you.

This is the nature of all successful attacks using the principle of our Tai Chi Chuan.

In essence, the victory goes to whoever is softer and better able to sense the intention of the opponent. Whether neutralizing or pushing, the principle is the same.

As for pushing, there is something of a debate among students of Professor Cheng's Tai Chi. "Is it possible," the question goes, "to propel someone a great distance without using the technique of stepping in on the push?"

Since Professor's death, most of the students studying his *gung fu* have only actually seen him on film and videotape. Much of his pushing on film shows him "stepping-in." As a matter of fact, he did often step in to enhance the power of his pushing, but he definitely did not teach, nor did he require, stepping-in as necessary in order to get a good push.

Stepping-in can be a useful technique. Once you have your opponent stuck, you can step to enhance the power of your *"tee fong"* (withdrawal/attack technique). Detecting the tell-tale wave of resistance, release slightly and then step through the opponent's center, thinking not so much of your hands but of your entire body moving through the opponent's center.

This is actually the spirit of the correct push, whether

you step or not: detect the resistance, withdraw slightly, and then come back through. The "withdrawal" serves to break the opponent's root while simultaneously allowing you to gather the energy from the ground. If you've done it correctly, you can propel him with tremendous force when you come back through. When you understand the technique, the idea of "enhancing" a really good push by stepping in almost boggles the imagination.

Some general stepping tips: First, never step in unless you have the opponent stuck, or you are just asking to get thrown off. Once you have them stuck, you can gather your rear leg up and then step through with your front foot; or simply release the front foot and step forward with it. In both cases, the opponent must not feel the movement in your hands. Your hands should be relating ever-so-lightly to his stuckness and "wave of resistance."

There's one more very cute and sneaky technique of stepping in: If you are confident about your control of your opponent, use his Push and your Rollback for the stepping-in. Wait until he has come forward as far as he can. While your weight is still on your back foot, sneak your front foot forward. Then, as he retreats and you advance—Surprise!—it's as if you're already in his backyard when he only expected you to be at the front door. The result can be exhilarating.

Again, he must not feel you do it, so you have to keep your hands light.

It's likely that if you depend on "stepping-in" for the key to a powerful push, you will not develop good pushing technique. First learn how to do it without stepping, to really understand the principle. Then add the step, and you can start your own personal air service, giving your opponents trips to distant places.

Speaking of distant places, films, and pushing, there is a very interesting film of a trip to Malaysia showing the great and fabled Huang Sheng-hsien in action.

The film shows Huang, in his seventies, giving a demonstration for a large audience. He reaches deep into his bag of tricks and reveals some pretty amazing stuff.

It shows him uprooting opponents. They fly away, but in his follow-through it seems as if Huang hasn't moved at all. After his opponents have sailed off, Huang remains like a statue, with his hands softly in pushing position; it's as if the opponent was pulled away by invisible ropes.

Even more amazing are a series of pushes where he doesn't use his hands at all. With one or more opponents pressing against him, he expands his *ch'i* and they are propelled off like corks powered out of champagne bottles.

There are some less dramatic, informative moments in the film—a brief section where Huang demonstrates the basic Push Hands form with one of his students, moving very quickly but without pushing. Huang and his student's hands and arms rapidly rotate around the pivot point of their elbows, which stay in absolute contact. It's significant that for all his formidable, almost mystical ability, Huang maintains his teacher Cheng Man-ch'ing's most basic technical element for the Push Hands: elbows in contact.

Another revealing section of the film shows Huang doing a version of that omnipresent exercise of Professor Cheng's, "The Bear." As he shifts his weight and turns his waist from side to side, Huang's arms swing up and down with the movement. His arms are impressive in their degree of looseness. They are like dangling ropes or well-cooked spaghetti, as if there is no bone in them.

After a minute or so of the exercise, a number of opponents charge at him and he repels them. After each push, he resumes the exercise, his arms as loose as before.

Huang is showing us a valuable idea. He could not be using those arms as loose as well-cooked spaghetti and maintain that looseness pushing against something unyielding like a wall.

You can only use softness to push something that's alive. Professor said: "You can lead a thousand-pound ox with four ounces, if you know the method, but you can't lead a thousand-pound stone horse." Huang has reached the level of "returning force," neutralizing and discharging almost simultaneously, at almost the same point in space and time. But his looseness implies cooperation with his opponent's force. For all the seemingly irresistible power, Huang is still going with the opponent's energy, not against it. That's the secret.

To the untutored eye, pushing—or discharging—seems to be overpowering opposing force. In fact, just as correct technique in following the opponent is to stick without pushing until they are stuck, pushing—discharging—itself is a heightened form of the same idea. *Tee fong*—"withdrawal/attack technique"—is in effect being able to "follow" the opponent through the subtle, brief events of what happens during the push.

As you follow an opponent, when they begin to get stuck, they will press back at you, subconsciously depending on you for support. At that first instant of resistance you yield, allowing the resistance to come toward you. This denies the opponent their expected support and breaks their root. Then, as the opponent rocks backward to try to recover their balance, you add to their energy as it moves away, discharging them. It happens in a very short space, in a small amount of time, but what seems to be "overpowering opposing force" is really sticking, yielding, and going with the energy.

Incidentally, an aspect of pushing that can be especially challenging is playing against an opponent who, when they start to get stuck, begin frantically twisting about in a fit of resistance. Professor had a simple suggestion for dealing with this odd behavior: "Just wait till they stop, then push them."

He also said, "Play Push Hands as if you are standing on the edge of a cliff." At first this seems a strange idea in an art that focuses on relaxing. How can you relax if you imagine yourself standing at the edge of a cliff?

One must consider the stakes. In Carlos Castaneda's early books, Don Juan is constantly telling his young disciple, "Your problem is, you think you're going to live forever. This is why you live so self-indulgently. If you want to understand how to live like a warrior, remember at every moment that Death stands behind your left shoulder."

We *are* standing at the edge of a cliff. Our problem is that we imagine we are not. We do our Push Hands talking about last night's party, or indulge our ego in hardness, waiting for some distant time when we hope to embrace *Tao*. We play Push Hands as we live—as if asleep, never waking up to the amazing, awesome one moment in our lives where we stand poised over eternity, aware that it is the only moment we will ever have, and that if we don't embrace it we have lost everything.

Self-Defense

When Professor began teaching in New York, Lou was one of his first students. With many years' experience in Judo and Aikido, Lou had the discrimination to realize that the *Tao* of Cheng Man-ch'ing was something very special.

One day he brought a young friend to meet Professor Cheng. Stanley was a heavyweight Judo player of championship caliber. At first glance he didn't look athletic—he was almost as wide as he was tall—but for all his tremendous bulk, he had a great sense of balance and was as quick as a cat. Like his mentor Lou, Stanley was more than a competitive Judo player, he was in love with the study of the martial arts.

Lou asked Professor to demonstrate some Tai Chi to Stanley. Professor took a Ward-off position and indicated that Stanley take his arm and attempt to throw him off-balance.

Stanley walked up to the old man and placed his hands on Professor's arm. After a moment, he released the arm and stepped back. Speechless for one of the few times in his life, Stanley looked quizzically at the old man for a long moment. Then he gathered his confidence and stepped in again, preparing to attack. After a moment, even more puzzled, he shook his head and stepped away.

"What's wrong, Stan?" Lou was smiling. "Why don't you see if you can push him off-balance?"

"What's the point?" Stanley answered. "He's got me from the second I touch him."

It took someone of considerable ability to be that aware of what he was confronted with, and Stanley went on to become one of Professor's finest students. Professor fondly named him "Chashu Bow," after the large Chinese roast pork bun.

This epic meeting of the Chashu Bow with Professor Cheng underlines the nature of Tai Chi as self defense: the *gung fu* expressed in immovable stability and irresistible sensitivity.

Recently an official of the weapons-control division of the New York City police department was asked in a published interview to estimate the number of teenagers carrying guns in the city. He guessed that approximately 50 percent of New York's teenagers carry handguns.

As students we must deepen the idea of *"Chuan"*—weaponless self defense—for it to function meaningfully in this kind of environment.

Obviously, it's most preferable not to have to fight at all. "In a fight," said Professor, "two things can happen. First, you can suffer the unspeakable: injury and even death. Second, and even worse, you can get in trouble with the law."

If a fight is unavoidable, the next alternative is the lesson of the sword, where the focus is to attack the wrist "so as to disarm the opponent." Nonviolence is one of the implications of the *Tao* that underlies Tai Chi—nonviolence not as abstract philosophy but as functional self-defense.

This seeming paradox becomes clear in Push Hands. Hardness in one tends to produce hardness in the other.

Angry resistance produces hostile pushes, and vice-versa. A virtue of keeping yourself soft is that it tends to soften the actions, psychology, and very energy of a potential opponent.

But there is still the possibility that for all your development of personal softness, you will one day have to deal with someone where "disarming" them does not diffuse their violent intent.

The fighting aspect of Tai Chi is most present in the form. Push Hands teaches lessons of sensitivity that enable us to use the martial tools of Tai Chi more effectively, but we develop and create those tools in the form.

The "Fair Lady Weaves at the Shuttle," the foundation of the *Da Liu* exercise, is a good way to explore self-defense applications. A hand comes striking at you. You catch it with your right hand, evade it by stepping back or turning; simultaneously extend it with your right hand and attack the elbow with your left elbow. Done correctly, you can snap an attacker's elbow like a twig. Or you can neutralize the elbow and step forward with your own strike.

Professor said about learning the technique of striking, "think of the opponent's body as being like a pane of glass. If you were trying to break a pane of glass, in order not to be cut, you would strike it sharply, with a whip-like or snapping motion, producing a shock wave that would break the glass.

"Hardness in an attacker makes their body brittle. You can learn to strike and shatter them inside as if they were glass. It's very terrible."

This image of the "glass" is where Push Hands and the form interface for fighting. Push Hands develops sensitivity to hardness and the center, the ability not to diffuse your power by locking it up with the opponent's resistance, but to be able to freeze them in time, like a video on pause, and then deliver your entire force at their vulnerable center.

But in Push Hands, you would use that understanding to uproot them. That is, in Professor's words, "much kinder" than using the tools of the form, where you would change the idea only slightly to "shatter them like glass." In Push Hands you attack their root; in striking you leave your energy in their body.

Normally, a Tai Chi player would take on a receptive attitude in the face of an attack, waiting for the opponent to make the first move. But in a situation where you have to initiate the attack, when you cannot afford to wait, such as having to deal with a group of attackers, the recommended technique is to attack first with a feint. When the opponent blocks in response, you then strike.

This is one of the basic principles of Push Hands. The opponent's block creates the same body rigidity—not only at the point of the block, but in their entire body's energy—that resistance creates in Push Hands. It is the resistance that gives you the opportunity to uproot in Push Hands; in fighting it is the rigidity that gives you something brittle to shatter. The technique of striking—breaking glass—is developed by making second nature postures like "Fair Lady," "Brush Knee," and "Press." Even the posture "Push" can be used either to strike or uproot.

There are no blocks in our Tai Chi because we want our bodies to be loose and soft, rather than hard and brittle— also for the effect of softness on the mind. To quote Professor Cheng:

> When you come to the point of having to defend your-self against a person who has a lot of strength and very fast hands:

When a Tai Chi adept is fighting, he will be able to control the other person and therefore be able to beat him. It's difficult to understand this. People with strength, people who have fast hands, don't believe in such a thing happening as what we are talking about.

How does it work? With this method of boxing you have to wait for the other person to move; then you will be able to take advantage of him. The opponent's strength is coming—I know, I realize it, I understand it—and then I can catch his strength, or receive it, just as you would catch a ball. This is the most difficult of all to understand. The hand and the foot come so quickly. How can you catch and control them? Everyone who looks at this particular idea thinks it is very strange.

Today I can clarify one aspect. Everyone pay attention: It is because we ourselves are very relaxed. Relaxed and very soft. So when an opponent comes to attack me with great strength and speed, I don't allow his hand to hit me. There's nothing there. "Before the opponent even thinks of moving, I already know what he's thinking. If you are not soft, you'll not be able to do this. If you are not relaxed, you'll never get there. The primary thing to remember in Tai Chi Chuan is to be relaxed and to be soft.*

As in Push Hands, "waiting for the other person to move" doesn't simply mean waiting for their physical movement. It relates to the ability to sense their energy before it expresses itself in movement. Whether *yin* or *yang*, forward or back, attack or retreat, the energy of the idea always precedes the action. There is tremendous advantage in being aware of what Professor called "impendence," the idea that precedes movement.

---

*Shr Jung Newsletter, Vol. 1, No. 3, 1976.

Tai Chi Chuan makes clear that sparring is not fighting and fighting is not self-defense. In the form there are none of the fighting stances beloved of so many other martial arts. There are only responses to an opponent's energy in the moment. According to the old man, a fighting stance means that you have signed a contract to fight, an action so stupid, he said, "that you deserve what you get."

A fighting stance indicates brittleness of body and mind; it is a commitment to a hard idea, contrary to the Tai Chi principle of softness and neutrality.

The strategy in a potential fight is to have no strategy. Your body should be relaxed, your mind neutral—"spacious as the universe." Don't project violent intent or violent nature, on the other. That is more likely to create what you want to avoid.

If your *ch'i* is strong, you have an even greater chance of defusing the anger and fear in a potential opponent. The greatness of your *ch'i* is also your best insurance against a mugger—it is the nature of a predator always to be drawn to the weak and disabled, never to attack the vital and powerful.

A very important point in the form is at the end. After completing the form, the next step you take is crucial for self-defense.

Is the next step Tai Chi Chuan, or is it off-balance, double-weighted, unaware, and unmindful of the chi?

You're walking down the street when suddenly a deranged derelict grabs at your arm. Do you freeze in fear, stiffen in anger, or do you behave like a Tai Chi player? "The next step you take at the end of the form," the habit it creates, will provide the answer.

Walk like a cat, weight dropping for power, eyes receptive, head pressed against heaven to have the spirit of feline alertness. In standing, be relaxed but always ready, with the weight on leg at a time. Standing with the weight evenly distributed, double-weighting, is stagnant. In sitting, don't slump. Professor said, "The back of the chair is to hang your coat. If you want to rest, lie down."

Sit with your back straight and your feet on the floor. Real *gung fu* would be to root, sitting without needing the chair.

Still, for all the transcendent self-defense ability one can achieve through Tai Chi Chuan, there are circumstances when it is appropriate to invest in loss—even to surrender.

One night, a senior student was robbed at knifepoint on the street. Confronted by the mugger, she simply handed him her purse and avoided any physical harm. Professor congratulated her for non-resistance, saying that she behaved like a true Tai Chi student. He said that if he had been in that situation, he would have done exactly the same. "Money is never something you should risk your life over," he said.

But the incident seemed to trouble him.

A few days later, he asked his assistants to search the city for a certain style of knife that he would have his senior students purchase, so that he could instruct them in its use. Soon a knife was brought to him for approval.

He was in his office. It was late, the classes were over, most of the students had gone home; a few senior students gathered around while he examined the weapon. He smiled and nodded; it was what he had in mind.

It was a vicious-looking thing, long and thin, only slightly smaller than a bayonet. Grinning, he began to play with it. "You're on a dark street and you sense someone coming up behind your right shoulder. Turn to face them by stepping in a curve to your left, rather than into the line of their advance," he said, surreptitiously reaching to his knife.

"If you see that they have a knife, don't be afraid. Think of it as a feather duster."

He showed us how to stand holding the knife completely hidden from an adversary by the back of the hand and the forearm.

"He doesn't know you have a knife, and he doesn't know where you will strike from." He could quickly change his grip to thrust from underneath or strike from above.

He leaped back with the dagger raised by his ear, his left hand extended in front of him. He stood poised, a killer. "If he still wants to fight after you've shown him this," he said murderously, "he deserves to die because he is too stupid to live."

It was like watching a Kung Fu movie. But the mood passed. He abandoned teaching the knife; it was rumored upon a lawyer's advice that the special knife course could create legal problems. He was careful to avoid "trouble with the law."

More likely, he probably realized that he had overreacted—the victimization of a woman was a touchy issue for him—and had simply come to his senses.

Psychological balance is much more important for self-defense than being able to send an attacker flying with a touch. With the never-ending incursion of difficult events and off-balance people into our lives, "defending oneself" is almost always a matter of knowing how to maintain balance and harmony in the face of the kind of attacks most of us usually have to deal with. Being good at Tai Chi Chuan does not mean being prepared for the one time in ten years that someone may actually physically attack you, while you allow yourself to be constantly battered and thrown by the daily challenges at work, in your family, in your life.

For all the adventure movies and Kung Fu films that present an image of "good guys" and "bad guys," the vast majority of difficult situations people suffer from result from the interrelationship of their own imbalance with the imbalance of their adversary. Your hard blow cannot strike home on my chest unless I stiffen it in resistance. My wife's accusation cannot drive me into a rage unless deep down I feel guilty.

The most effective form of self-defense is learning to remove the buttons that my myriad of daily "attackers" push to throw me off-balance. I must learn to relax my fear and guilt.

In a world where teenagers carry handguns, and where soon atomic weapons will be in the possession of all nations, and all their ethnic and religious subgroups, and eventually perhaps even neighborhood block associations, it would be very good to develop Tai Chi players able to practice and teach the ability not to see their own fear reflected in the faces of people who are different, Tai Chi players who have learned the true secret of self-defense.

Grandfather Yang's Back

The trunk should be straight and not tilted. The backbone and the tailbone should be aligned like a plumb line.

The joints of the arms should be loose at all times. The shoulders should sink, with the elbows slightly bent and the palms naturally straight, sitting on the wrist. The ends of the fingers should be slightly bent. Use your mind to move the arms. Let the *ch'i* fill the fingers. After days and months of the accumulation of this kind of practice, the inner energy will begin to make itself felt.*

Little is more unique to Professor Cheng's Tai Chi than the quality of the arms—most specifically the hands and wrists. The "sitting wrist" is a reference to the idea of the hand and forearm being one piece, without any break in the wrist. But there are pictures of Grandfather Yang doing the form that show much more angularity in the wrist than Professor's characteristic "Beautiful Lady's Hand" with its gently curved wrist.

As a matter of fact, the same pictures reveal a generally harder-looking form. Yang Cheng-fu's back leans forward where Professor's spine is straight; his sacrum hasn't dropped like Professor's, and his back leg is not bent.

---

*Excerpted from "Special Points about Five Parts of the Body" by Yang Cheng-fu.

Professor always quoted Grandfather Yang, saying that the spine should be "straight as a plumb line." When he was asked about the discrepancy between these well-known pictures of Grandfather Yang and the basic postural principles he said he had learned from Yang Cheng-fu, Professor answered, "These pictures were taken before Grandfather Yang had deepened his understanding of Tai Chi, before he had developed the ideas we are practicing."

The "Beautiful Lady's Hand" has a special place for Cheng Man-ch'ing: "There are no secrets, but if there were ..." it begins with the Beautiful Lady's Hand.

The characteristic of li energy, "hard force," is heavy hand and light elbow. The hand and arm exert force from the shoulder.

Soft, *chin* energy is the opposite: light hand, heavy elbow. With the hand soft and the elbow hanging heavy, the hand and arm can only channel the energy of the body rather than issue it independently from the shoulder. It's like the bumper of a car: The movement of the car provides the force; the bumper only channels it.

Professor said that the major task in the study of Tai Chi is to take hard force out of the hand and arm. Once you do, you enter the parlor of Tai Chi.

Yang Cheng-fu's advice to "let the *ch'i* fill the fingers" is one of the classic methods. You cannot exert hard force with the hands at the same time your heart-mind sends *ch'i* into the fingers. It's the same as in Push Hands, where you cannot both push and listen at the same time.

"*Ch'i* in the fingertips" is also great for your health. The fingertips are like the nozzle of a hose. If the water is coming out of the nozzle, it's circulating through the entire hose. In this case, it's the *ch'i* that is moving without blockage if it's pouring into the fingertips.

Professor taught a few other ideas which help develop *ch'i* in the fingertips while at the same time taking away the hard, stiff force from hand and arm.

"Treat the air like water," he said. "Tai Chi is also known as dry-land swimming because of this idea. If you can begin to treat the air around you as having weight and substance, you will develop the resiliency of a small child and your *ch'i* will be very powerful. The more you relax, the more you will be able to feel the air like water; the more you feel the air, the more you will relax."

Decades of "treating the air like water" has a very positive martial effect, though for Professor it also had an unexpected complication. He told us it was difficult for him to discipline his children. "I have to use a hair brush," he said. "If I tried to paddle them on the behind with my hand, I would injure them because of my chi."

Another helpful image for developing *ch'i* is "Drawing Silk From a Cocoon." Professor said, "Once you start to draw out the silk you must continue drawing it out evenly. If you speed up, the silk will tear; if you stop and start again, it will break. You must draw it out at the same constant, even tempo."

Another name for Tai Chi is "Long Boxing." Professor had created his thirty-seven posture form from Yang Cheng-fu's original form of over 100 postures. He took exception to those who referred to his innovation as the "short form." He explained, "The form we study is not the short form. It is the 'Long Form with thirty-seven postures.' Tai Chi was based originally on only thirteen postures which themselves were called 'Long Boxing' because they flow endlessly, without stopping, like the Long River."

Doing the form "Like the Long River," or "Drawing Silk" is an important method of *ch'i* development. Beginners especially need to focus on this idea since the postures are taught as a series of tableaus, contrary to the principle of "Long Boxing."

There's another image which I learned from an experienced doctor of acupuncture, Madame Gu. Describing the difference between the traditional and modern study of acupuncture, Dr. Gu said, "It used to be that before you learned to place the needles, you had to master the *ch'i*. It sometimes could take thirty years. One of the ways you learned was that you stood by a well and raised and lowered your hands. When the water in the well would rise and fall with your hands, then you were ready to learn where to put the needles." This is great image for the opening posture, for "putting the *ch'i* into the fingertips." Raise and lower your hands as if you were standing by a well, raising and lowering the water.

If the stories about of the mastery of "chi in the fingertips" sound like fairy tales, they await a commitment to "decades of practice" to discover. One of my favorite stories is one Professor Cheng told about "the other time" he "played" with Yang Cheng- fu.

He went up to Grandfather Yang and asked him about the application of the first part of the Single Whip. They were in the courtyard where Professor had had his previous stunning experience with his fierce teacher.

As Professor told the story, Grandfather Yang placed his hands palm down on Professor's wrists. Then he turned and Professor said he had become attached to his teacher's palms, so that when Yang turned Professor stumbled around like a helpless puppet.

Yang turned back and once again Professor was dragged along, as if irresistibly magnetized. The third time Yang turned, he released Professor, who was thrown with such force that it knocked him unconscious.

Considering his experiences in "playing" with his teacher, Professor seems to have been fearless in the pursuit of knowledge.

Grandfather Yang
on Defining Weight

It is most important that the legs be clearly defined as to which is the weight-bearing and non-weight-bearing. When walking you should lift and lower your legs lightly, like the paws of a cat. When the weight is totally supported by the left leg, the right leg will have the ability to move freely, as quick as the mind itself. As to the method of dropping weight into the weight-bearing leg: you shouldn't use effort to press your weight into the leg; instead, with your backbone straight, lower your body at the hip joint as if you were sitting down. Let the lower part of the leg be almost perpendicular to the ground. If it's bent too much at the ankle, the body will tilt forward or backward and lose its balance.*

The quality of cat-like walking to which Yang Cheng-fu refers is difficult to achieve but quite beneficial. The way people walk "normally" is actually controlled falling. They don't really stabilize themselves in the leg that supports their weight. In the process they are off balance and, in effect, need to catch themselves from falling with each step. If one wishes to be "centered" on a spiritual or psychological level, it would be helpful not to be off-balance in standing and

---

*"Special Points About Five Parts of the Body," by Yang Cheng-fu.

walking, some of the most fundamental states of our lives.

Every step we take will be balanced and centered if we learn the principle of "weight totally supported in the weight-bearing leg."

After working on the idea for some time, I had a clear insight one night when walking in the dark. I unexpectedly stepped into an electric cord strung across my path. Because I had been walking "like a cat" I felt the cord and drew my leg back. I also realized that had I been moving the way I used to, with my weight committed into the step, I would've tripped over the wire and had a nasty fall.

In one of his Eight Methods, "Walking on Ice," Professor Cheng supplied his students with a good method of practice. The Eight Methods are a series of simple exercises which he devised to help those who because of age or illness couldn't do the basic form. The Eight Methods can benefit anyone.

"Walking On Ice" teaches "cat-like walking." Professor Cheng described the image: "Imagine you are walking across a frozen lake. You don't know how solid the ice is. Each step could break through the ice. If you place the foot down with weight in it, you could fall through the ice to your doom. Therefore what you have to do is carefully place each step with absolutely no weight in it. Roll your weight into the foot. Then sit down in that foot and extend the next step with the foot completely empty. Repeat the process with each step until you have crossed the lake."

Another of the Eight Methods that helps one to walk like a cat is "Wearing the Moon for a Hat." Here the idea is to walk as if the round ball of the moon is on your head. If you are not straight, if your movement is not smooth and level, the "moon" would fall off your head. Practicing this idea helps with balance and alertness in one's movement, in addition to being great for the health.

Yang Cheng-fu's advice "not to use effort to press your weight into the leg" also applies to rooting practice. Rooting is one of the most important parts of developing *gung fu*, but the student should sit down and concentrate on relaxation and alignment. Then the "weight dropping" will happen on its own. "Pressing the weight down" is a hardness that has the opposite effect: hardness always produces a light floating-away-from-the-ground rather than a heavy dropping-into-it.

Not using force for the weight, breath, or postures is one of the clearest lessons Professor Cheng received from Grandfather Yang. It also is the difference between Professor and so many other teachers. Whenever a student presented him with a Tai Chi idea they heard somewhere that promised great benefits but required some kind of forcing, hardness, or rigidity, he would always warn against it.

In rooting, the empty leg is often not paid enough attention. "Tai Chi" means the polarity of empty and full; one of the basic health benefits of Tai Chi Chuan is the way it can enhance cardiovascular circulation.

In Western medicine the legs are called "The Second Heart." Strengthening and toning the muscles in the legs helps the heart circulate the blood. As people age, their leg muscles deteriorate so that blood tends to pool in the legs, causing all sorts of problems. But the circulation doesn't just benefit from strong leg muscles. Even more helpful is Tai Chi's goal of strenuously working one leg while totally relaxing the other; alternating effort and relaxation makes for cardiovascular health. Therefore, practice "emptying out" the non-weight-bearing leg while thinking about filling up the weight-bearing leg.

Besides sitting on one leg at a time, "defining the weight" has to do with the principle of double-weighting. In the application of Tai Chi Chuan the understanding of "double-weighting" is essential. In doing the form, and later in Push Hands, we must be aware that the soft *chin* energy, always flows from the ground, through the weight-bearing leg and up the back, and is finally channeled out by the hand opposite the weight-bearing leg. In other words, if the weight is primarily on the left leg, the *chin* energy will emerge from the right hand, and vice-versa. Attempting to release energy contrary to this principle—say using the left hand while the weight is on the left leg—is called "double-weighting" and, along with hard, stiff force, to which it is related, is a major "no-no" in Tai Chi Chuan.

Professor said, "Do the form as if someone is there; do Push Hands as if no one is there." In Push Hands that means don't let more than four ounces of force build up on you, nor allow yourself to build up more than four ounces on the opponent.

For the form, "Doing the form as if someone is there" does not mean thinking in terms of punching people, at least not initially. If you start your study with that kind of idea, you will bring your habits of hard force to the practice. Our first job as students is to use the form to totally relax, and learn to get rid of all stiffness and hard force.

The next stage is to develop the internal, soft *chin* energy. Play the form thinking about energy flows from the ground, through the weight-bearing leg to the opposite hand, at every point in the postures. It will always shift, as the weight shifts, emerging from one hand and then the other.

However, it's not quite that simple. Some years ago, two students were practicing Push Hands. One of them, Lenny, now a senior student at Long River Tai Chi, was having a lot of trouble with an opponent who had more physical strength.

"Why is it?" Lenny protested. "I have my weight on my right leg, and I'm pushing him with my left hand. He has his weight on his left leg and he's pushing me with his left hand. And he's pushing me over! He's double-weighted and I'm not. In terms of what you've told us about Tai Chi, I should be winning, not him."

It was time to tell Lenny another secret. In fact, they were both double-weighted, and in that case it's simply a matter of strength. So the stronger—Lenny's opponent—would win. Having weight on the right leg and using the left hand does not mean you are not double-weighted; it only means you are in position not to be. The *chin* energy "Sprouts in the Ground," through the weight-bearing leg and out the opposite hand. If you have not developed root, learned to relax into the ground and use its energy, it doesn't matter which leg you are on, you are still using the strength of hand and arm. What "double-weighting" really means is that the energy is not sprouting in the ground.

But if your weight is on your left leg and you use your left hand to try to release energy, basic physics makes it impossible not to be double-weighted.

Practice Push Hands, and especially the form, contemplating deeply the ideas of "differentiating weight" and "double-weighting." When the understanding is a part of you—not when you have to pause and think about it, but when in releasing energy you would no sooner "double-weight" than you would step in front of a moving bus—at that point you've become a Tai Chi boxer.

Footnote from
Three Generations

There are two applications of the sole of the foot. One is to kick with the toes. In this instance the mind should be at the toes. The other is to hit with the heel. In this case the mind should be on the entire sole. For where the mind is, the *ch'i* comes; where the *ch'i* is, the inner energy comes. The joints of the legs should be loosened. The easiest time to make the mistake of using stiff, hard force is when you are kicking. When you fall into this error, the body will be unbalanced and the inner energy will not flow through the kicking leg.*

Professor Cheng often referred to Grandfather Yang's warning about kicking. He told a story about an old friend who was also a Tai Chi student. The fellow had been very sickly before he started the study of Tai Chi. After a few years, his health improved markedly, along with a growing ability in Tai Chi.

Then Professor started to notice that though the fellow seemed to be practicing diligently, his health had begun to deteriorate. He questioned him closely and discovered that the man had gotten it into his head to, as he put it, "learn how to really kick someone," and he had been using a lot

---

*"Special Points About Five Parts of the Body," by Yang Cheng-fu.

of hard force in his kicking. "Everything else he was doing was correct," said Professor, "but the hard force in the kicks destroyed the virtue of all the rest of his practice." He went on to explain that developing *ch'i* in each round of form is cumulative: the further you go into the round—provided it is one continuous flow, without a break—the more *ch'i* you are developing. If you break the round, either by stopping and starting, or through tension or hardness, the *ch'i* development stops. Then, when you begin again, it's like starting at zero.

The kicks are the place where there is the greatest tendency for the practitioner to use hard, stiff force. It is also the place where students have the most trouble relaxing. Because of their fear of falling, students often tighten up and stiffly try to hold on to the sky to keep from toppling over.

It's difficult to have faith at that point, to let go and relax when fear of falling seems to drive the body to tighten up. Professor Cheng's tool of "investing in loss" has as much value in the kicks as it does in Push Hands. There is great benefit if one can yield one's ego, relax, and "let go of the sky" at this most challenging point in the form.

Time of practice: Each and every day, twice after you get up in the morning and twice before you go to bed. In one day you should practice seven or eight times at least. But if you get drunk or eat too much, it's better not to practice for a while after.

The best place to practice is in a garden or a large hall where there is plenty of light and sunshine. You must avoid direct wind, wetness, or foul air. Because when you are practicing, you must breathe deeply so it's easy for wind or foul air to get deep into you. That will harm your lungs or internal organs and cause sickness. If you are short of space, Tai Chi Chuan can still be practiced in an area 3' x 3'."*

Years ago, when I showed Bob Smith the work I'd been doing with this writing of Yang Cheng-fu, he made a startling observation about "time of practice." "You know," Bob said, "when Yang Cheng-fu says practice seven or eight times, it's the long form he's referring to, approximately twenty minutes to a half-hour."

When students of Tai Chi talk about the need to supplement their practice with jogging, biking, or other aerobic activities, I ask them how long they practice each day. Generally their answer is, "About a half-hour."

A half-hour of daily practice is very good for one's health. It oils the hinges in the morning after you wake up, lets everything start to flow and gives you a base of relaxation to support the stresses of the day. At night, you can relax the body and mind from the day's accumulated tension so you don't have to carry it into sleep.

However, *gung fu* means that "you get out what you put in." If you want to take the exercise past the daily maintenance level of a round of "Professor's long form with thirty-seven postures" in the morning and night, if you want your Tai Chi to continue to grow and deepen, two to three hours of practice a day is not unreasonable. A serious tennis player or runner would not be put off by that regimen, and practicing Tai Chi is more accessible and a lot less taxing than the same amount of "aerobic" exercise.

It's interesting that recent research on heart disease suggests that HDL, the so-called "good cholesterol" which

---

*"Special Points About Five Parts of the Body," Yang Cheng-fu.

flushes out the "bad" LDL, accumulates more from duration of exercise than intensity. A person taking a three mile walk in a relaxed hour produces higher levels of HDL than one who does the same hike in a high intensity half-hour. Professor Cheng's admonition to "enjoy your practice" might also be a factor.

As regards "place," Professor said it was somewhat inconsistent to live in the city and practice Tai Chi Chuan, because of how bad the air is in urban centers.

"If you are so unfortunate as to have to live in a city like this," Professor said, "make sure you spend a lot of time in the park." On this account he heeded his own advice. He lived right next to Riverside Park, and often walked there.

He told us how at times he would sit at his window, look out over the park and the river, and draw inspiration for his painting and poetry. He might dream of clouds drifting across the sky back home, or think of the lotus flower that gave him one of his names, "Father of the Lotus."

He said that the air in the city was not simply inferior to clean country air. "It's not the same," he said. "It's completely different.

"When you are able to get to the country, or someplace where the air is good, take advantage of it. Open yourself to the air. But when you are in bad air, it's important that you close yourself to it."

This advice seems difficult, but as we deepen our breathing, learning to "guard the *ch'i* with our heart-mind in the *tan tien*," it is less forbidding.

The well-known phrase "Tai Chi Chuan can be practiced in an area 3' x 3'" has puzzled a lot of students. It requires knowing the principle of the "jailhouse form," as we called it at Shr Jung school.

Though you may need a teacher to help with the fine points, the basic idea is that any time a foot is completely weightless, it can be placed anywhere. Then there will be no "break" in the flow, and the chi-developing quality of the round will be maintained. Familiarity with the choreography of the form helps in "jailhousing," because you usually need to think ahead to make the adjustments in foot position.

Doing the "jailhouse form" is a less than ideal way to practice, but it has its particular benefits, most of all as a lesson in "differentiating weight." Since you have to move the "empty foot" more often than in a normal round, it will inform you whether the empty foot is completely empty and the weight 100 percent in the other foot.

Another benefit of the "jailhouse form" is that it helps a class or group of students stick together through a round of form. If a person at the perimeter should meet a wall, he needs to "jailhouse" in order to keep his form from breaking its flow. At that point, the person behind him will need to adjust, and so on.

Professor told us that the Tai Chi in his New York school measured up very well with that in China. Hopefully, it's still true, but when I see films of practitioners in China doing their Tai Chi together, if I don't necessarily envy their general level of *gung fu*, I am almost always impressed with their quality of "sticking together" as a group doing the form.

Tai Chi asks an individual to develop two seemingly contradictory characteristics. On one hand, we must learn to "do our own thing," in the most basic sense—learn to let go of all our tension and armor to realize our true nature, an aspect of the greatness of our *ch'i*. On the other hand, there is the requirement to let go of our ego so that we can "stick" to the movement and energy of another, the martial application. In sticking together as a group, students of Tai Chi are building the foundation for the higher levels of the art of sticking, "understanding energy."

The energy used in other martial arts is called 'the muscular energy developed after one's birth.' Before birth a foetus has inner energy and *ch'i*. At birth the infant cries and takes in its first breath of external *ch'i*. From then on most people use this muscular, external energy more and more, and their internal energy and *ch'i* less and less.

The application of external, muscular energy has a beginning and an end. Therefore there is a moment, for instance, when the action of throwing a punch has been finished, the energy has stopped, and a new action hasn't yet started. During that split-second there is a gap where the person using external energy is vulnerable. But when you use internal energy, your spirit is always ready; the everpresent spirit and *ch'i* provide the motivation, and there is no gap in the energy for others to use to their advantage.

Seek quietude in the movements. Practicing other martial arts involves the use of all of one's strength, so after practice one is usually out of breath.... Tai Chi Chuan uses the stillness of the mind to direct the movements. Even in performing the movements there is quietude. In quietude the movement is controlled so that your breathing will be long, deep and fine. The *ch'i* will sink into the *tan tien* and from there permeate your body. Thus there will be no stiffening of the limbs, joints and blood vessels, and you will never get out of breath.*

There is an illusion in learning form and Push Hands with an eye to "function," the martial application. It is nec-

---

*"Ten Important Points for Practicing Tai Chi Chuan," by Yang Cheng-fu.

essary to progress along a path developing certain technical abilities—pushing, neutralizing, striking, locking—but
when one reaches a certain level in the accumulation of *ch'i*
and internal energy, those same technical abilities lose their
relevance and fall away, like a snake shedding its skin. One's
being becomes an expression of *ch'i* and spirit.

Professor told a story of walking with Yang Cheng-fu
when a strongly built, aggressive person bumped into him.
The fellow bounced off Grandfather Yang and fell to the
ground. He got up and glared, but Grandfather Yang continued walking, wrapped in conversation, as if unaware that
the fellow had even touched him.

Yang Cheng-fu and Cheng Man-ch'ing were very different. Yang was rough and uneducated; Professor Cheng was
artistic, highly educated. What was the bond that joined
them?

One of Professor Cheng's famous old students, T. T.
Liang, compared himself to his teacher, "Cheng Man-ch'ing
is Master of Five Excellences: calligraphy, painting, poetry,
chess, and Tai Chi. His skills are above standard.

"I have Five Excellences, too: Gambler, Drug Addict,
Alcoholic, Opium Smoker, and Spendthrift. Five Excellences.

"His excellences, though, were really different than
mine."*

Old T.T.'s joke strikes to the heart of what it was that
united Professor and his teacher, Yang Cheng-fu.

It certainly was not culture. Yang's "excellences" were
probably closer to T. T. Liang's than Professor's. But *Tao* is
neither about higher education nor street-wise experience.

Full Circle Magazine (Vol. 1, No. 4, Nov. 1986, Boulder, CO)

Neither one gives any special advantage. As a matter of fact, in a basic sense we are all dealt the same hand of cards for the game of opening the Gateway to the Miraculous. Born with a silver spoon, born in the ghetto; healthy, crippled; all have their unique qualities, advantages, and disadvantages in terms of "the game."

Success awaits a particular kind of effort—*gung fu*—that anyone can apply, and that is equally difficult, no matter who you are and where you come from.

Can you let go of your tension and hardness? Can you embrace what remains?

T. T. Liang's version of Professor's "Five Excellences" got one wrong: Though Professor was an excellent chess player, the fifth "excellence" was medicine, not chess.

It is very clear from the study of the writing of Yang Cheng-fu how similar he and Professor were. Perhaps the one significant difference between them had to do with Professor's art of medicine. The health benefit of Tai Chi Chuan was its foremost virtue, as far as Professor was concerned. Every aspect of Professor Cheng's Tai Chi Chuan is to develop the flow and accumulation of one's *ch'i.* "Concentrating one's chi" for the resilience of a small child is his definition of good health, the benefit from which all the benefits of Tai Chi are gained.